ONE DEVOTION A DAY FOR GIRLS

BARBOUR kidz
A Division of Barbour Publishing

Print ISBN 979-8-89151-134-7

Published by Barbour Publishing, Inc., 1810 Barbour Drive, Uhrichsville, Ohio 44683, www.barbourbooks.com

Our mission is to inspire the world with the life-changing message of the Bible.

Printed in China.
002513 0625 HA

DAY 1

Remember to do good and help each other. Gifts like this please God.
HEBREWS 13:16

Christmas is so exciting! Wrapping presents, whispering secrets, sampling cookies—what's not to love? But did you know that your gifts don't have to cost money or come wrapped in pretty paper and bows? You can give amazing gifts to God and others without spending a dime.

God says one of the best gifts you can give is kindness expressed in good deeds and help. Does your mom need help around the house after a long day? Give the gift of loading the dishwasher or folding a load of laundry. Does your friend need help with their homework in your favorite subject? Give the gift of explaining a difficult concept to them. Hold open a door for someone. Rake your elderly neighbor's leaves. Share your things. Collect canned foods for a food bank. Make friends with the new kid. Sneak a special snack to someone who really deserves a treat.

God smiles on these acts of kindness to others. And as a bonus, you'll feel great too!

God, show me who needs my kindness today. Amen.

DAY 2

WATCH YOUR STEP

When you are around people who do not know God, be careful how you act. Even if they talk against you as wrong-doers, in the end they will give thanks to God for your good works when Christ comes again.
1 PETER 2:12

It's great to be liked, to fit in, especially with our friends. But sometimes trying to be accepted by other people instead of living to please God can lead you to do the wrong thing. You might be afraid someone will laugh at you or stop being your friend if you don't join in with their wrong behavior. They might even accuse *you* of being wrong!

But the Bible says to be careful not to sin or behave wrongly around people who don't know God. Instead, be an example of God's goodness, kindness, and love with your actions and words. Your friends might just ask why you are different. And then you can tell them that you love others because Jesus loves you—and even better, He loves them too!

Heavenly Father, help me do the right thing and tell my friends about Jesus, even if someone makes fun of me. Amen.

DAY 3

LET IT GO

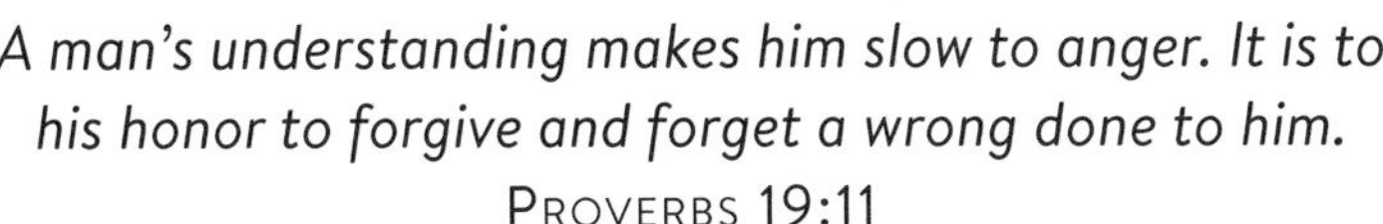

A man's understanding makes him slow to anger. It is to his honor to forgive and forget a wrong done to him.

PROVERBS 19:11

Why is it so hard to forgive sometimes? Forgiveness usually means that someone has hurt us—even if they've just hurt our feelings with careless or unkind words. Forgiving someone doesn't mean that you think what they did is okay or right. It just means you choose not to allow your hurt to make you sin by holding on to anger or trying to get back at the other person.

The Bible says it is honorable to overlook a wrong done to you. In other words, let it go! You can choose not to be offended or respond with mean and angry words or actions—you can be kind instead. Pray about your pain and God will give you comfort.

Remember that often people who say and do mean things are hurting inside. And they need the love of Jesus to help them heal too. Show them Jesus by forgiving.

Is there someone you need to forgive?

God, help me let go of my anger and forgive others. Amen.

DAY 4

BE CAREFUL WHAT YOU SAY

A fool always loses his temper, but a wise man keeps quiet.
PROVERBS 29:11

What do you do when you get mad? Is there someone you know—a sister or brother, someone at school, a friend or cousin—who is always getting under your skin? Do you say mean things to them? Or how about when your parents don't give you what you want. How do you react? Do you argue, yell, and stomp to your room?

God says you're wise to show self-control, even when you're angry—*especially* when you're angry. You can still obey your parents without a disrespectful attitude and speak gently to others when you're upset.

Anger itself isn't wrong. It's usually what happens next that gets you into trouble. Anger becomes wrong when we do wrong things because of it—losing control, yelling, slamming doors, or saying hurtful things. Guilt and regret always come next.

Before you open your mouth in anger today, stop and pray. Ask God to help you practice self-control by keeping those angry words quiet. You'll be so glad you did!

God, help me control my temper so I don't say hurtful words to others. Amen.

DAY 5

LIVE JOYFULLY

Our hope comes from God. May He fill you with joy and peace because of your trust in Him.
Romans 15:13

You get a new bike. Your mom says you can have a sleepover with your best friend. Your dad buys you ice cream to celebrate a big win. It's easy to feel joyful when things are going well for you. But what about when they're not?

What if your little sister breaks your favorite necklace?

Or your parents tell you no when you wanted them to say yes *soooo* bad?

Or your best friend says something hurtful to you?

God can fill you with joy even in the not-so-good times. And He will if you ask. When you trust in Jesus, He fills you with the hope of an amazing future with Him—and that is something to smile about.

When you're feeling down, turn on some praise music, list all the good things God has given you, and ask Him to change your feelings. He will show you all the reasons you have to be joyful!

God, fill me with joy, even when things don't go the way I want. Amen.

DAY 6

SPEAK TRUTH

Do not lie to each other. You have put out of your life your old ways.
COLOSSIANS 3:9

Telling the truth can be tough—especially when you've done something that you know is going to get you into trouble. But when you follow Jesus, He wants you to take off your old ways of doing things and put on new ways—His good and perfect ways.

The Bible says that God hates lying but He delights in those who tell the truth. He feels this way because lying damages your relationships. It breaks trust. And broken trust is hard to fix.

Satan, your enemy, is the father of lies. And he is happy anytime he can get you to lie too. Next time you're thinking about bending the truth, ask yourself, *Who do I want as my father? The Father of truth or the father of lies?* Beat the enemy today by always telling the truth. And your heavenly Father will be delighted with you!

Father, give me strength to always tell the truth, no matter what. Amen.

DAY 7

THE RIGHT CHOICE

"Choose today whom you will serve. . . .
But as for me and my family, we will serve the Lord."
JOSHUA 24:15

Life involves lots and lots of choices. The little ones, like picking a color to wear today, don't mean too much in the big picture. But there are also important choices that can make a huge difference. We choose which friends to spend time with and what activities will fill our day. We choose which foods we will eat. To obey our parents. Or to disobey. To be kind or rude with our words and actions. Which TV shows we will watch and what music we will listen to. And we choose whether to spend time reading our Bible, or not.

It's important to stop and think about who you are serving with your choices. Are you choosing to serve God by doing what is right and good? Or are your choices leading you into the enemy territory of sin?

The sum of all your little choices becomes your character. What are your choices saying about your character? Are you choosing things that please God?

Heavenly Father, help me choose to serve You today and every day. Amen.

DAY 8

PRAY TODAY

I love the Lord, because He hears my voice and my prayers.

PSALM 116:1

Did you know that God always hears your prayers? He does! Unlike your friends or your parents who are sometimes distracted, God is always listening. And He will never tell you to wait just a minute. In fact, He wants to talk to you. Every day! All day!

The Bible says to pray continually—that means all the time. You don't have to use big or flowery words. You don't have to talk out loud or be in church. You don't even have to close your eyes. Praying is simply talking with God and listening for what He has to say back. It's a conversation with the one who created you, who loves you very much.

You can talk to God about everything. If you're worried, tell God about your fears and ask Him for peace. If you need help making a decision, ask God for wisdom. If you're lonely, talk to Him—ask Him to send a friend your way. He always answers.

Father, I want to spend more time talking to You—about everything. Amen.

DAY 9

PRICELESS

*"I have called you by name. You are Mine! . . .
For I am the Lord your God, the Holy One of
Israel, Who saves you. . . . You are of great worth
in My eyes. You are honored and I love you."*
Isaiah 43:1, 3–4

One-of-a-kind paintings hang in the Louvre Museum in Paris—like Leonardo da Vinci's *Mona Lisa*. These fabulous works of art were crafted by master artists and are worth a fortune.

Did you know that you were also crafted by the Master Creator—the God of the whole universe? He shaped every part of you to be exactly how He wanted you to be. He gave you your unique personality, your special talents and interests. And just like there is only one *Mona Lisa*, there is only one you. God says you are of great worth to Him, and He loves you because you belong to Him.

Just like those priceless paintings on display in museums, your value comes from the one who made you. Because you were created by God, you are worthy. You are loved.

Lord, thank You that I am valuable because You made me. Amen.

DAY 10

NO WORRIES!

Do not worry. Learn to pray about everything. Give thanks to God as you ask Him for what you need. The peace of God is much greater than the human mind can understand. This peace will keep your hearts and minds through Christ Jesus.
PHILIPPIANS 4:6–7

School, chores, sports, music lessons, homework, clubs, and church programs—your schedule is packed. And sometimes stress and anxiety can attack even when you're having fun. The newness and change of growing up can be scary and stressful too.

But the apostle Paul wrote that you shouldn't worry about anything. Not. One. Thing. Why? Because you can have peace in your heart, knowing that your God is really big and can handle the huge job of taking care of you.

So how can you trade your worry for peace in the middle of this busy, scary life? The Bible says to pray about everything and ask God to take care of what you need. He will help you! And don't forget to thank Him for all the things He's already done for you.

**God, fill me with Your peace.
You've got this. I give my worries to You. Amen.**

DAY 11

A BEAUTIFUL SPIRIT

Do not let your beauty come from the outside. It should not be the way you comb your hair or the wearing of gold or the wearing of fine clothes. Your beauty should come from the inside. It should come from the heart. This is the kind that lasts. Your beauty should be a gentle and quiet spirit. In God's sight this is of great worth and no amount of money can buy it.

1 PETER 3:3–4

A new dress. A fresh hairstyle. Painted nails. A pretty smile. What things come to your mind when you think of someone who is beautiful? Usually we think of things that are on the outside. But the Bible tells us that God sees deeper than that. He looks at your heart.

No matter what you look like on the outside, you can be beautiful to God. Someday you'll grow older and maybe your skin will get wrinkled and your hair will turn gray, but the kind of beauty that lasts forever—the beauty that God sees—is gentleness, kindness, and a calm and faithful trust in the Lord.

Lord, help me to be beautiful on the inside. Amen.

DAY 12

POISONOUS PRIDE

"Those who have no pride in their hearts are happy, because the earth will be given to them."
MATTHEW 5:5

Have you ever been really good at something? And maybe a sneaky feeling crept over you that your talent made you just a little more important? Or maybe you have nicer clothes or live in a bigger house than some of your friends and you feel as if you're a little bit better than they are.

Watch out for pride. It's the opposite of how God wants you to behave. Jesus gave us a perfect example of being humble. He is the Son of God, yet He didn't think Himself too good to serve others by washing their dirty feet.

Remember that every person you meet is just as valuable to God as you are—this thought will keep you thinking right about yourself and how you treat others.

Heavenly Father, keep me from becoming puffed up with pride. I know that I am precious to You, just like each and every person I'll meet today. Amen.

DAY 13

DO THE RIGHT THING

Do not let yourselves get tired of doing good. If we do not give up, we will get what is coming to us at the right time. Because of this, we should do good to everyone. For sure, we should do good to those who belong to Christ.
GALATIANS 6:9–10

Sometimes doing the right thing is hard. You know you should finish your chores, but you really want to watch your favorite TV show or paint your nails instead. And you know that talking about one of your friends behind her back isn't right, but all the other girls in your circle are joining in. Will you choose God's way?

God says not to get tired of choosing to do the right thing, even when it's hard. Just keep doing the right thing in every situation. Read your Bible every day so you know what God says about how you should live.

And remember, making choices that are pleasing to God comes with rewards! Not only will you build good character, but you'll also pile up heavenly rewards.

Father, give me strength to do what is right, every time. Amen.

DAY 14

HE LOVED YOU FIRST

We love Him because He loved us first.
1 John 4:19

Jesus loves you—no matter what! He knew you and loved you before you were even born. In fact, He came to earth to die for your sins long before you were alive. Think about it. He gave up His life for yours—now that is true, unselfish love!

Even if you've messed up and done the wrong thing, He still loves you. Even if your friends turn against you, He still loves you. Even if you feel alone, He loves you still. If you haven't accepted Jesus as your Savior, you can pray and tell Him right now that you love Him too and want Him to forgive your sins and come into your life.

It's easy to love Jesus, because He loved you first. And He always will. Know that you are loved today, and share His love with everyone you meet.

**God, thank You for loving me first.
I can't earn Your love or lose it,
because it's already mine forever. Amen.**

DAY 15

FOLLOW THE GOLDEN RULE

"Do for other people whatever you would like to have them do for you."
MATTHEW 7:12

Someone says something not so nice about you, or cuts in front of you in line, or ignores you. What do you do? What do you think Jesus would want you to do?

If you're not sure what Jesus would say, you can find out by looking in your Bible. He said to treat other people the way you would like to be treated. That makes things so simple! We all prefer to be treated with kindness over rudeness and selfishness.

It's easy to be kind to people who are already kind to you, but it's much harder to be nice when someone is mean to you or hurts your feelings. But you aren't responsible to God for their actions, only your own. Too often people who treat others poorly are hurting inside. So treat them with the kindness you desire. Your gentleness may be just the bandage they need for their pain, and they may even start to change their ways.

Heavenly Father, when someone isn't nice to me, help me to show them Your love. Amen.

DAY 16

THE NEW YOU

You were chosen to be free. Be careful that you do not please your old selves by sinning because you are free. Live this free life by loving and helping others.

GALATIANS 5:13

Before you knew Jesus you probably did whatever made you feel good. But now you know Jesus and how much He loves you. He forgave you for every wrong thing you've ever done and every wrong word you've ever said. You're free from all that guilt! Jesus has changed you into a brand-new you!

But you are probably in the habit of doing things the way you always have. And bad habits—like thinking of yourself first—are hard to break!

Jesus wants you to live in freedom—the freedom to love others and help them. It might seem really hard to stop acting like the old you, but you have a great helper! God will help you if you ask.

Is there a bad habit you need to break?

Father, help me to break old habits that are wrong and to be able to live free to love others. Make me brave and strong so I can love even when it's hard. Amen.

DAY 17

GOD'S WAY FIRST

"First of all, look for the holy nation of God. Be right with Him. All these other things will be given to you also."
MATTHEW 6:33

Have you ever come down with a case of the gotta-have-it bug? "Mom, I've got to have a new pair of shoes." "I really, really *need* these new jeans." "But my friends have. . ." You fill in the blank with whatever it is you are wishing for.

Things are nice, and new things can be exciting. But God doesn't want us to spend all of our time chasing stuff. In fact, He says we don't even have to worry about having stuff—He will give us everything we need. Notice He doesn't say everything we *want*.

Instead of craving everything you could buy, God wants you to spend your time looking for His way of doing things. He wants you to do right, love others, and be generous. Trust Him to take care of your needs. He will!

Father, help me want to do the things that please You. I trust You to give me what I need. Amen.

DAY 18

WHAT ARE YOU THINKING?

Take hold of every thought and make it obey Christ.
2 CORINTHIANS 10:5

Did you know that everything you do starts with a thought? That includes both right things and wrong. The Bible tells us to be careful what we spend our time thinking about and to catch all the wrong thoughts and lock them up, just like the police put the bad guys in jail so they can't cause trouble.

Your enemy, the devil, is happy when you are thinking wrong thoughts. But you can beat the devil! Just ask yourself if what you're thinking about is right. Does this thought make God happy, or the devil?

If you're wondering why you should please God, the Bible says that Satan is here to steal and kill and destroy. He's not the kind of friend you want! But God loves you and wants to give you good things when you listen to Him. He is the best friend who always does what's best for you.

Check your thoughts today. Would they make God smile, or do they need to be locked up?

Father, help me to see when my thoughts are wrong and change them into right thoughts. Amen.

DAY 19

BE BRAVE

"Be strong and have strength of heart. Do not be afraid or shake with fear because of them. For the Lord your God is the One Who goes with you. He will be faithful to you. He will not leave you alone."

DEUTERONOMY 31:6

It can be hard to be brave when you're all alone. But if a friend goes with you, suddenly you feel so much more courageous! The Bible tells us to be strong and have courage because God goes with us. Everywhere you go God is always there with you. That's what it means to be faithful—to never leave! And God is faithful to you. That means you'll never be alone!

Sometimes we need to be brave to do the right thing—like helping out a friend or being kind—even when no one else is. God is bigger than your fears. He helped David bring down a giant, and He can help you too. So even if your fears seem greater than a giant, give them to God and ask Him to give you faith and courage.

Lord, help me to trust You and be brave. Give me strong faith like David's. Amen.

DAY 20

NEW CLOTHES

Therefore, as God's chosen people, holy and dearly loved, clothe yourselves with compassion, kindness, humility, gentleness and patience.
COLOSSIANS 3:12 NIV

I bet you've never jumped out of bed when your alarm beeped, eaten your breakfast, and run out the door—only to realize you forgot to put your clothes on! Getting dressed is important. So we do it every day, almost without thinking.

But do you ever forget to put on your patience when you are getting ready for the day? Or how about your kindness? Do you rush around frustrated when you have to wait on your food, your parents to take you somewhere, or an answer to a question? Do you consider the feelings of others?

God thinks these good things are even more important than what you're wearing on the outside. Start every day right. Remember your most important accessories—compassion, kindness, humility, gentleness, and patience.

Father, You love me so much. Help me remember that my clothes are not as important as my actions. Amen.

DAY 21

HAPPY HELPER

Whatever work you do, do it with all your heart.
Do it for the Lord and not for men.
COLOSSIANS 3:23

What kind of chores do your parents ask you to help out with at home? Do you make your bed, fold your laundry, or feed your pets? Part of growing up is learning how to be responsible—that's just a big word that means Mom and Dad can count on you!

Growing into a responsible girl takes a lot of hard work. Sometimes you may not feel like doing the things you are asked to do. What should you do if you feel this way? Should you grumble and put off finishing your chores?

It can help to remember that God says to do every job with all your heart, as if you were doing it for Him. It doesn't matter whether you're finishing your homework or washing the dishes, smile and do your best—you're working for your Father in heaven.

Lord, help me to have a happy and willing heart as I finish every job. Amen.

DAY 22

BE AN OVERCOMER

Do not let sin have power over you. Let good have power over sin!
ROMANS 12:21

Sometimes bad things happen, even to good people. And it can seem as if the bad is always winning: Bullies pick on kids at school, people steal, unkind gossip is more popular than an encouraging word. But God has a way for you to become an overcomer.

The Bible says that Jesus has already overcome this world—He died to free you from being trapped by sin. He wants to help you show the world how good can have power over evil.

Ask God to help you resist the temptation to do the wrong thing—even if all your friends are choosing sin. Stand up for good. Be an example of how kind words can overcome hurtful words and how compassion for others can overcome selfishness. With God's help you can be an overcomer! Jesus is praying for you to win against evil.

Heavenly Father, make me strong to overcome evil with good. Amen.

DAY 23

MAGNIFICENTLY MODEST

Christian women should not be dressed in the kind of clothes and their hair should not be combed in a way that will make people look at them. They should not wear much gold or pearls or clothes that cost much money. Instead of these things, Christian women should be known for doing good things and living good lives.
1 Timothy 2:9–10

God wants His girls to be modest. He wants people to notice you for all the good you do instead of for how good you look.

Taking care of yourself is also important to God. He loves you and doesn't want you to be dirty or unhealthy. But He does want you to know that doing right and living to please Him is more important than getting attention because of the way you look.

Your clothes aren't the only way you can be modest. You can also be modest in your behavior by having a calm and gentle spirit. He doesn't want you to get wrapped up in drama or throw fits when you're upset. How can you be modest today?

Lord, show me any areas where I need to have more modesty. Amen.

DAY 24

NO PROBLEM TOO BIG

"The Lord will fight for you. All you have to do is keep still."
Exodus 14:14

Have you ever had a problem that just felt too big for you to fix? One where you seemed so small and helpless beside this big, impossible thing?

Did you know that the Israelites felt this way after they escaped slavery in Egypt? They were backed up against the Red Sea with no way across and Pharaoh's army was chasing them. The situation seemed hopeless.

But nothing is hopeless for God. He is bigger than all of your problems. When the Israelites thought there was no way, God parted the sea and they walked across on dry land.

God will fight for you too. When you are feeling hopeless, pray and ask God to take over. Trust Him to care for you and give all your worries to Him. You can rest, knowing that the same God who parted a sea can solve your problems too.

God, I trust you. Help me to stop worrying and let You do the work. Amen.

DAY 25

LOVE ALWAYS

"I give you a new Law. You are to love each other. You must love each other as I have loved you."
John 13:34

What exactly does it mean to love like Jesus?

Loving like Jesus means putting others in front of yourself, forgiving those who have hurt you, doing good for people—even people who don't like you—being kind, and having compassion. It means loving with everything you've got!

That sounds like a big job. And honestly, loving all the time is hard work. So why should we do it? The short answer is because Jesus loves *us* this way, and He asks us to follow His example.

Jesus showed us in the Bible how to love other people, no matter what they look like or where they live. Jesus was never selfish. He always thought about what other people needed and how they were feeling. And He wants you to do the same!

You can do it—with His help!

Jesus, thank You for loving me all the time, no matter what. Show me how to love others like You love me. Amen.

DAY 26

KIND

You must be kind to each other. Think of the other person. Forgive other people just as God forgave you because of Christ's death on the cross.
Ephesians 4:32

You walk into a room full of other kids, but you don't know anyone there. You feel nervous and afraid that no one will want to be your friend. Then one of the girls comes over and says, "Hi, my name is Amy. What's yours? Do you want to come sit with me?"

How would her kindness make you feel? Doesn't it feel great when someone is kind to you?

Now think about how you could make other people feel that way inside too. All it takes is a little kindness. If you don't know how, remember. . .just treat others the way you would like to be treated. Your kindness just might inspire your friends to be kind too.

Think about how you could show kindness to your parents, grandparents, siblings, and friends. What act of kindness could you do today?

God, show me who needs my kindness today. Give me courage to be kind. Amen.

DAY 27

A GIVING GIRL

Tell them to do good and be rich in good works. They should give much to those in need and be ready to share.
1 TIMOTHY 6:18

Are you a sharer or a saver? Do you often give away your things to others, or do you keep them to yourself? God wants us to be generous with what we have. After all, He is the one who gives us everything we need, and He wants us to pass it on!

Try sharing today! Be generous and see how God will reward you with blessings—even if that means the blessing of feeling good inside because you helped another person or made them smile with your gift.

And God isn't just talking about your stuff when He says to share. You can be generous with your time too! Stop and hold open a door, help an elderly neighbor mow their grass or rake their leaves, or help your parents with extra chores.

How can you be generous today?

Lord, thank You for everything You have given me. Help me to give back and help others. Amen.

DAY 28

STRONG WITH JESUS

I can do all things because Christ gives me the strength.
PHILIPPIANS 4:13

When the apostle Paul wrote these words, he was sitting in prison for telling other people about Jesus. Sometimes doing what you know God wants you to do can be really hard, especially when following Jesus means that something not-so-nice might happen to you.

But this verse means that we are not all alone in the hard times. Jesus sees you when you obey Him, and He will make you strong to do what He asks. If you are kind to an unpopular kid at school even if your other friends are making fun of her, Jesus sees you and will help you to be strong and keep on doing good.

How do you need Jesus to help you be strong in your life? Do you need His strength to keep a good attitude when you have to do chores? To obey your mom and dad when you'd rather not? To be kind? To tell your friends about Jesus?

What hard thing could you do with Jesus' help?

God, give me Your strength today to do the right thing. Amen.

DAY 29

STAY POSITIVE

Be glad you can do the things you should be doing. Do all things without arguing and talking about how you wish you did not have to do them.
PHILIPPIANS 2:14

What is your response when your parents or a teacher asks you to do something you don't really want to do—like clean out your hamster cage or write a report? Do you grumble? Complain? Whine? Argue? Or maybe you say, "Sure, I can do that!"

God wants you to have an attitude of thankfulness all the time. Instead of wishing you didn't have to do some things and thinking about what you'd rather be doing, try being thankful that you *can* do what you're asked.

It's super easy. It goes like this: *Thank You, God, for giving me this furry little hamster to cuddle.* Or *Thank You, God, that I am able to go to school and learn to write when lots of kids in the world can't go to school.* Or *Thank You, God, that we ate such good food off of these dishes that I'm washing.*

Try it today! You'll be singing while you work.

Lord, show me how to be grateful instead of grumbling. Amen.

DAY 30

GIVE GOD HONOR

Whatever you do, do everything to honor God.
1 Corinthians 10:31

Have you ever collected something—like dolls or rocks? If you collect rocks, then you've probably spent a lot of time thinking about rocks, looking at rocks, and getting more rocks. Your collection might not be worth a lot to someone else, but in your mind it's priceless.

Honor works the same way. To honor something or someone means you have given it worth in your life. To honor God means that the way you live shows that He is valuable to you.

So how do you honor God with everything you do? None of us are perfect, so at times we're all going to mess up. But you can honor God by always thinking about what He would want you to do. Make choices that please God by doing what the Bible says is right.

And God is even more pleased when you honor Him in your heart. That means you *want* to do right not just because your parents make you, but because you love God and think He's precious and a must-have in your life.

Lord, help all my choices show that I love You. Amen.

DAY 31

LEARN SELF-CONTROL

A man who cannot rule his own spirit is like a city whose walls are broken down.
PROVERBS 25:28

Why did ancient cities have strong walls around them? To keep their enemies out, right? So if a city's walls were falling apart, the people who lived there would have no protection. Their enemies could walk right in and take over. The people of the city would have their property stolen and they might even end up as slaves.

So why does the Bible compare broken-down city walls to our self-control? Because when you use self-control in the choices you make, it's like a strong wall of protection around your life to keep out your enemy—Satan.

When you choose to do the right thing, even when it's really hard, instead of allowing yourself to do something wrong—like not whining when your parents ask you to do something, or not spending time with friends who are doing or saying bad things—you're using self-control! Don't become a slave to doing the wrong thing! Build strong walls of self-control today.

God, make me strong to control myself and choose right over wrong. Amen.

DAY 32

THE RIGHT FRIENDS

He who walks with wise men will be wise.
PROVERBS 13:20

"You become who you hang out with." You might have heard this saying before, and the Bible tells us the same thing—you will be like the people you spend time with. Your friends will influence you, so it's important to choose good friends.

When you're choosing your close friends, ask yourself, *Is it a wise choice to hang out with this person? Will this friend encourage me to follow Jesus?* You should stay away from people who do and say things that go against what the Bible teaches us is right; otherwise they could lead you away from Jesus—and into harm.

Choosing not to spend time with some people doesn't mean you think you're better than they are. God loves them too! And He died for their sins just like He died for yours. So pray for them to come to know Jesus too.

Pick friends who are kind, loving, joyful, compassionate, patient, and giving—and you will become more of those things too!

Lord, give me wisdom as I choose who to hang out with. Send me friends who love You. Amen.

DAY 33

THANK GOD FOR WHAT YOU HAVE

Keep your lives free from the love of money.
Be happy with what you have.
Hebrews 13:5

Have you ever watched a commercial on TV for a toy. . .and then told your parents you just had to have it? New stuff can be fun. But the Bible tells us not to get all wrapped up in everything we could buy. God says to be happy with what we have.

The problem with wanting everything you see is that when you're so busy longing for all the things you *don't* have, you aren't enjoying the things you actually *do* have. Being content lets you enjoy all the wonderful things God has already given you.

The next time you're feeling like you really, really *need* to have something, ask yourself if you believe that God has given you everything you need. Is there anything that you actually *need* that you don't have? Then list some of the things God has supplied for you—and thank Him for all the wonderful things you have.

God, thank You for always being there for me and for giving me so much. Amen.

DAY 34

OTHERS FIRST

Nothing should be done because of pride or thinking about yourself. Think of other people as more important than yourself.
Philippians 2:3

Thinking about yourself is easy. We want to do and have what we want. And we want it first! But God tells us to think about other people. Have you ever let someone else choose first what TV show to watch, or shared a snack that you really wanted to eat all by yourself? If you have, awesome job! You've learned to put others before yourself.

Jesus doesn't want us to be selfish and think of ourselves all the time. He wants us to give willingly to others—just like He did.

The next time you're tempted to hold back and keep something to yourself, just ask: *Am I putting the other person first, or am I being selfish? What is the kind and generous thing to do?*

Follow in Jesus' footsteps and give! You won't be sorry you did!

Heavenly Father, it's hard not to be selfish sometimes. Help me to put others first. Amen.

DAY 35

SPEAK GOOD THINGS

Watch your talk! No bad words should be coming from your mouth. Say what is good. Your words should help others grow as Christians.
EPHESIANS 4:29

You've probably heard someone say, "Sticks and stones may break my bones, but words can never hurt me." It's a nice thought, but if anyone has ever said something mean to you or teased you, you know how much words actually *can* hurt.

God wants us to be very careful about the words we say, because He knows we can really hurt each other by saying unkind things. And He has a different job for your words! God says to build others up and encourage them with your words instead of tearing others down.

Your challenge for the day is to say only encouraging and helpful things to your siblings and friends. Build them up and help them follow Jesus with the words you speak. Your words are powerful—use them for good and not for evil!

God, show me when my words are not helpful. Put kind and encouraging words in my mouth today. Amen.

DAY 36

YOU'RE UNIQUE!

A heart that has peace is life to the body, but wrong desires are like the wasting away of the bones.
PROVERBS 14:30

Have you ever thought you weren't as good as one of your friends? Maybe you thought she was better because she got better grades. Or maybe she was better at sports or dancing. God says not to compare yourself to others. In fact, the Bible says these kinds of jealous thoughts are like rotten bones!

God spent time creating you just how He wanted you to be. He gave you talents that are unique to you. You're special in your own way! And God wants you to use all those special gifts for Him.

Instead of wishing you were like someone else, thank God for being so creative and making you different and special. Think of things you're good at—maybe you're a good leader, or make friends easily, or enjoy helping others—and ask God how He wants you to use those talents today.

God, help me not to compare myself to others. Show me how I can serve You with my talents. Amen.

DAY 37

ASK FOR WISDOM

If you do not have wisdom, ask God for it. He is always ready to give it to you and will never say you are wrong for asking.
JAMES 1:5

What makes someone wise? Does it mean they make straight A's in school or know the answer to every question? Not exactly.

Wisdom is different from being super smart. It means you make good decisions. A wise girl takes time to think about her choices before she decides what to do. Wisdom also means doing the things that please God—because wisdom comes from God.

Yep! That's right, God is the source of wisdom. So if you're in need of some wisdom, all you have to do is ask God. He promises He will give it to you. Studying your Bible also helps you to make wise choices because it tells us what God says is right. Open your Bible today and gain some wisdom!

Lord, give me wisdom in the choices I make.
I love You and want to do what You say is right. Amen.

DAY 38

PLEASE GOD NOT PEOPLE

Happy is the man who does not walk in the way sinful men tell him to, or stand in the path of sinners, or sit with those who laugh at the truth. But he finds joy in the Law of the Lord and thinks about His Law day and night.

Psalm 1:1–2

Have you ever done something you knew was wrong because your friends were doing it? Maybe you didn't want them to laugh at you or stop being your friend because you didn't join in. That's called peer pressure.

But God says you won't find joy by sinning right along with everyone else. Maybe you need new friends! God says you will find joy in His ways and the things He says are right. You'll find joy by walking with Jesus and doing good!

God wants you to think about His ways all the time, not just on Sunday at church. That means reading your Bible every day and living like Jesus wherever you are. Live to please God instead of your friends and you will have true joy!

God, make me strong to do the right thing, even when it's not popular. Amen.

DAY 39

FIRST IN SERVING

"Whoever wants to be first among you, let him be your servant. For the Son of Man came not to be cared for. He came to care for others."
MATTHEW 20:27–28

Important people have lots of servants to do stuff for them, right? *Hmm.* The princess dream *is* pretty popular, but being a princess in God's kingdom doesn't mean you get the royal treatment.

In fact, Jesus tells us it means just the opposite. He says if you want to be first in His kingdom, you should follow His example and serve others. The servant life doesn't seem very glamorous, does it? So why should we work to help other people?

We love others because of God's amazing love for us! He forgives us always and gives us grace we don't deserve—for free!

So how can you serve in God's kingdom today? It's easy! Find a person and see what they need. And then help them! Be kind. Give generously. Love unselfishly.

Lord, help me not to be selfish so I can be first in Your kingdom. Amen.

DAY 40

STUDY HARD

"This book of the Law must not leave your mouth. Think about it day and night, so you may be careful to do all that is written in it. Then all will go well with you. You will receive many good things."
JOSHUA 1:8

How do you think you would do on your next history test in school if you never opened your history book and read it? Probably not great, right? It's the same with following Jesus. How will you know what choices you should make or what behaviors will please God if you never open your Bible and read it? You can't!

The Bible says to study and think about God's directions all the time so you'll be careful to do what is right instead of what is wrong. Go get your Bible and open it. Spend some time reading what God says about how to live a life that is pleasing to Him. He loves you and wants your life to go well!

Heavenly Father, show me the right way to live as I read Your Word. Amen.

DAY 41

LOVE HIM

"You must love the Lord your God with all your heart and with all your soul and with all your mind and with all your strength."
MARK 12:30

Have you ever decided to do something because someone else wanted you to? Maybe your dad wanted you to play soccer, but you didn't really like it. Or maybe your friend asked you to take ballet with her, but it wasn't really your thing. Since you didn't want these activities for yourself, you probably didn't work super hard at them.

But maybe you love drawing. All day long you see everything around you in pictures. You think about the colors you could use, the lines you could draw. And you spend all your energy and extra money on all things art.

God wants you to be that devoted to Him, to love Him with everything you've got. Because He is worthy! He is the Creator of this world—and you! He is good and trustworthy. And He loved you enough to send Jesus to die so He could spend all of eternity with you.

Father, I want to love You today with all of my heart, soul, mind, and strength. Amen.

DAY 42

PLAN FOR PEACE

Those who plan peace have joy.
PROVERBS 12:20

Sometimes we all enjoy a little excitement in our lives, especially when good things are happening—like a special vacation or your birthday. But some people seem to get the wrong enjoyment over causing trouble.

Do you know anyone who loves to stir up drama? Maybe they spread rumors or make things that happen sound worse than they are just to get everyone upset. They seem to enjoy starting arguments over getting along.

Drama is exhausting, and the Bible tells us to work toward peace. God doesn't want us to have fun by causing trouble. He says when you work for peace, you get joy. Just think of how easy and fun it is when you're getting along with your friends.

The next time you're tempted to add a little drama, ask yourself, *Am I trying to have peace with my friends, siblings, and parents? Or am I stirring up trouble?* Be a peacemaker instead of a drama queen. The reward is joy!

God, help me to work for peace. Amen.

DAY 43

TRY GOD'S WAY

"Do what is right and good in the eyes of the Lord. Then it will be well with you."
DEUTERONOMY 6:18

It probably seems like everyone is always telling you how to behave—do this, don't do that. And sometimes you just feel like doing what *you* want to do. So you might be wondering why you should do what God says.

The most important thing to remember is that God loves you! More than you can ever imagine. And He is good—all the way through. He's not trying to control you or trick you. He loves you so much that He wants only what's best for you. And because He is the powerful God who created both this world and you, you can trust Him to know what's best.

When you do the things that God says are right and good—like being kind, helping others, and forgiving—you can be sure that things will go better for you than if you try to do stuff your way.

Try it today. Live God's way and see how life starts looking up!

God, help me to do what You say is right and good. Amen.

DAY 44

WHEN YOU'RE FEELING SAD

We give thanks to the God and Father of our Lord Jesus Christ. He is our Father Who shows us loving-kindness and our God Who gives us comfort. He gives us comfort in all our troubles.

2 Corinthians 1:3–4

What do you do when you're feeling sad? Do you get a hug from Mom or Dad? Have a good cry? Eat your favorite food or watch a funny TV show?

Have you ever asked God to help you with your pain? He can comfort you no matter what kind of trouble you're in. If you think that no one understands your sadness, He does.

Jesus knows all about pain. He was betrayed by His friends, made fun of, beaten, and killed. People He loved died. And He saw others who were hurting and sick. He can understand your sadness and hurt too.

Pray and tell Jesus how you feel. Ask Him to bring you comfort. Read your Bible and learn about how you can trust God because He loves you. Talk to your parents or another grown-up who loves Jesus.

Jesus, I'm so glad You understand how I feel. Help heal my hurt and sadness. Amen.

DAY 45

YOUR HELPER

I pray that because of the riches of His shining-greatness, He will make you strong with power in your hearts through the Holy Spirit.
EPHESIANS 3:16

God wants His girls to be virtuous—that means "good." He wants you to make wise choices, treat people with kindness and love, and serve others. . .even when it's hard.

Doing the right thing all the time might sound impossible, but God will help you! In fact, He has given you a secret weapon. When you follow Jesus, the Holy Spirit comes to live in your heart. The Holy Spirit is your helper. In the Bible Jesus even called Him the helper. And He can help to make you strong so you can choose to do the right thing.

Rely on the Holy Spirit today! The next time you find it hard to do what is right, pray and ask the Holy Spirit to make you strong and give you the power to choose good.

Lord, I want to be virtuous and do what You say is right, but I'm struggling right now. Please make me strong with the power of Your Holy Spirit so I can do the right thing. Amen.

DAY 46

KEEP TRYING

Do not give up. And as you wait and do not give up, live God-like.
2 Peter 1:6

Do you remember when you were learning how to write the letters of the alphabet or how to tie your shoes? Did you think you would never get it right? But do you *still* think that writing the letter *A* or tying your shoes is impossible? Probably not, right? I bet you don't even have to think about it anymore, and you do it perfectly!

It's the same with doing the right thing. It takes practice. The more you choose to do what is right—like sharing, or obeying your parents right away, or saying encouraging words to others—the easier it becomes to make good choices.

So don't be discouraged if you mess up sometimes! Or even if you mess up a lot when you first try to choose right over wrong. After all, the ABCs you wrote in kindergarten were much messier than what you can do now. Don't give up. Keep practicing how to do right!

Heavenly Father, please forgive me when I mess up, and help me keep trying to do right. Amen.

DAY 47

GOD'S DIRECTIONS

Man is helped when he is taught God's Word. It shows what is wrong. It changes the way of a man's life. It shows him how to be right with God. It gives the man who belongs to God everything he needs to work well for Him.
2 Timothy 3:16–17

You got a new game from your friend, and you were so excited to play it—but when you set up the board and pulled out the pieces, you discovered that there were no directions to tell you how to play. What could you do? Of course you wouldn't know what to do with all those pieces or how to win the game!

The Bible is like those game directions for your life. It tells you everything you need to know about who God is and what's right and wrong. And it also tells you how to live with Him in heaven forever—by believing in Jesus and asking Him to forgive you and make His home in your heart.

Read your Bible right now! God can't wait to show you how to live for Him!

Lord, help me read my Bible every day so I'm ready to work for You. Amen.

DAY 48

NEVER TOO YOUNG

Let no one show little respect for you because you are young. Show other Christians how to live by your life. They should be able to follow you in the way you talk and in what you do. Show them how to live in faith and in love and in holy living.
1 TIMOTHY 4:12

You've probably heard the words "Maybe when you're older" more often than you'd like. Waiting to grow up can be hard. But guess what? You're not too young to work for God!

The Bible says you can work for Jesus no matter how young you are. You can be a good example of how to live for God. You can be kind and choose encouraging words that please God. You can love others by helping out—and doing it with a happy heart!

Other people will see your good example and learn how to live for God too! How can you work for God today?

Father, show me the work You want me to do for You today. Help me to show others what is right by the good choices I make. Amen.

DAY 49

YOU WIN!

"He who has power and wins will receive these things. I will be his God and he will be My son."
REVELATION 21:7

Has your team ever won at sports? Or maybe you were victorious at checkers or the fastest one in a race. Doesn't it feel great to win?

Did you know that God wants you to win too? The Bible tells us that through Jesus we have *already* won the victory!

You might be wondering what kind of victory it is that Jesus has won for us. He won when He died on the cross for your sins. When you know Jesus and ask Him to come into your heart, you are forgiven and become part of God's family. You win because the wrong things you have done no longer keep you away from God. You win because the Holy Spirit now lives in you. You win because as a daughter of God, you will live forever with Him in heaven.

Lord, help me to remember that You have given me the power to do good through the Holy Spirit and the victory through Jesus. Amen.

DAY 50

PATIENCE, PLEASE

But they who wait upon the Lord will get new strength. They will rise up with wings like eagles. They will run and not get tired. They will walk and not become weak.
Isaiah 40:31

"Good things come to those who wait." Or at least that's what Mom and Dad have probably told you when you were impatient for something to happen. But waiting can be so hard! Even grown-ups struggle with waiting sometimes.

But did you know that God says if you wait for Him, He will do the work for you? Have you ever seen a bird soaring higher and higher into the sky, but it wasn't flapping its wings at all? It didn't need to do all that work flapping because it was riding the wind.

When you wait for God and pray for Him to show you what He wants you to do, He will carry you along to His good plans for you—just like the wind carried that bird.

God, waiting is hard. I want to run ahead and do what I want. Give me patience to wait for You. Thank You for giving me energy so I can do what You ask. Amen.

DAY 51

DON'T GET TRICKED BY TEMPTATION

"Watch and pray so that you will not be tempted. Man's spirit is willing, but the body does not have the power to do it."
MATTHEW 26:41

"Watch out!" Has someone ever shouted a warning at you to keep you from getting hurt? Maybe you weren't paying attention and almost stepped out in front of a car, but your friend pulled you back.

Just like we watch out for danger, God says to watch out for temptation. Because temptation can be sneaky—like when you think something is good, but it's actually bad.

Maybe you thought telling a "little lie" to get yourself out of trouble was okay. Or that talking about someone behind their back wouldn't hurt anyone. Don't be tricked by the devil into doing wrong!

But sometimes even when we know something is wrong—like doing what your parents told you not to—we still want to do it. We can't resist temptation by ourselves. We need God to make us strong. And we need our Bibles to help us know what's really right.

God, I don't want to get tricked by temptation. Help me to look out for sin and choose right. Amen.

DAY 52

HAPPY TO SHARE

Nothing should be done because of pride or thinking about yourself. Think of other people as more important than yourself.
PHILIPPIANS 2:3

You grab all of the best stickers and glitter pens for your craft, only to see your little sister's sad face when she realizes there aren't any left for her. You got exactly what you wanted, but then you realize that getting it all to yourself did not make you feel good inside.

Can you really be happy when what you've done has made someone else feel bad? Sharing and giving up something you really want is hard, but you will feel so much better inside if you do!

God always wants us to put others first instead of thinking about ourselves all the time. Sharing is one way that you can be a good example and show God's love to other people. After all, God shared His Son, Jesus, with us. So you can show how thankful you are for all that God has given you by sharing with others!

God, help me not to be selfish. Show me what I have that I could share with others today. Amen.

DAY 53

GENTLE JUST LIKE JESUS

A gentle answer turns away anger,
but a sharp word causes anger.
PROVERBS 15:1

In Bible times God's people, the Jewish people, were waiting for a king who would come and fight their enemies in a big battle, conquer them, and rule over them. But when Jesus came, He was a different kind of king. Instead of fighting, Jesus said, "Learn from Me. I am gentle and do not have pride. You will have rest for your souls" (Matthew 11:29).

Jesus wants you to be mighty in gentleness too. When someone laughs at you or pushes you or takes something that's yours, the first thing you probably want to do is yell at them and get mad. But God says that speaking gentle words will calm both your temper and theirs.

You can defeat anger and fighting with gentleness. Ask God to help you not to speak sharp words today!

Jesus, teach me how to be gentle like You.
Help me to stop arguments and fighting
by using my gentleness. Amen.

DAY 54

BE UNDERSTANDING

Try to understand other people. Forgive each other. If you have something against someone, forgive him. That is the way the Lord forgave you.
COLOSSIANS 3:13

Have you ever gotten upset about something because you didn't know the whole story? Maybe you were mad at your best friend because she forgot to text you, only to find out later that she'd gotten sick and needed to rest. Or maybe your little brother spilled your paint on the floor and you yelled at him—but then your mom told you he was trying to make you a birthday card.

We should always have forgiveness in our hearts. And when we stop thinking about ourselves and try to understand other people, forgiveness comes much more easily. After all, you are a pretty great girl in God's eyes, but you're still not perfect. And that means you need forgiveness sometimes too.

Next time you start to get upset at someone, stop and think. There might be more to their story. God always forgives, and so should you.

God, help me care about others and try to understand their problems instead of getting angry. Help me to always forgive. Amen.

DAY 55

WITH A HAPPY HEART

"These people show respect to Me with their mouth, but their heart is far from Me."
MATTHEW 15:8

If you do what your mom asks, but you stomp away and complain the whole time, are you really being obedient? Not so much, huh? That's because your heart isn't in the right place.

Did you know that God can see your heart? It's true. He can! That means that He can see if your attitude is right. And you can't fool Him—He knows why you do things.

God doesn't just want you to say the right things when you're at church; He wants you to love Him in your heart. And when you love Him, you'll want to please Him by doing what the Bible says is right!

It's true that we don't earn His grace and love by the things that we do—He loves us anyway. But when we love God with our whole heart, we have joy and want to please Him because He is an awesome God who loves us!

God, I want to be real with You.
Keep my attitude pure. Amen.

DAY 56

SHED THAT SELFISHNESS!

Jesus said to His followers, "If anyone wants to be My follower, he must forget about himself. He must take up his cross and follow Me."
MATTHEW 16:24

Jesus is the best example of being unselfish. He didn't just give up a pair of shoes He liked or a favorite snack—He gave up His life. If you are following Jesus, there should be more of Him and less of you in your life. In other words, you are becoming more like Jesus.

God knows your heart—even the thoughts you don't tell anyone else. Are any of those thoughts selfish? Do you have places in your life where you could be more selfless? Places where you could put others in front of yourself or think more about how other people feel?

It's so easy to be selfish because we're all sinners. That's why we have to fight hard against Satan and not allow selfish thoughts to tell us how to act. Instead, ask God what He wants you to do.

How can you make "You go first, I'll go last" your motto today?

Lord, please show me when I am selfish and help me to become more like You. Amen.

DAY 57

WALK WITH INTEGRITY

He who is right in his walk is sure in his steps,
but he who takes the wrong way will be found out.
Proverbs 10:9

Integrity is a big word that means "choosing to do the right thing all the time". . .even when no one is watching.

Have you ever noticed that when you do something wrong, your heart is full of worry, hoping no one finds out? Or you end up telling a lie to cover up what you did. So much stress, just because you tried to hide your wrong.

But if you choose to do right, you can have sure steps. No stress. No worry about being found out. And besides, you never really get away with doing wrong, because God is always watching. You can't fool Him. He always knows.

Choosing sin never makes you feel good inside—instead, it brings guilt and worry. But choosing what is right will put joy in your heart. Become a girl of integrity. Others will know they can trust you to do the right thing—all the time!

God, help me to be someone others can trust to always do the right thing. Amen.

DAY 58

SHOW GOD'S KINDNESS

The king said, "Is there not still someone of the family of Saul to whom I may show the kindness of God?" And Ziba said to the king, "There is still a son of Jonathan who cannot walk because of his feet."
2 Samuel 9:3

In Bible times, when one king conquered another kingdom, he would often get rid of the family of the losing king. But King David wasn't that kind of king. He chose kindness instead.

Even though King Saul had tried to kill him, when King David found out that Saul's grandson Mephibosheth was still alive, David took care of him.

Meanness (or being selfish and angry) happens a lot. Usually when someone is mean, you want to be mean right back. But with God's help you can be a different kind of girl. One who chooses to be kind. . .even when others aren't.

How can you show God's kindness to someone who hasn't been nice to you?

Lord, make me strong in kindness like King David. Amen.

DAY 59

SHARE THE GOOD NEWS!

We thank God for the power Christ has given us. He leads us and makes us win in everything. He speaks through us wherever we go. The Good News is like a sweet smell to those who hear it.

2 Corinthians 2:14

The yummy smell of cinnamon rolls makes you jump out of bed and scurry to the kitchen as fast as you can. Mom made your favorite treat for breakfast!

God says that the good news of Jesus is just like a sweet smell. When you tell others about Jesus' love for them, it sounds so good that they will want to know more—just the way those cinnamon rolls make your mouth water for more!

The news that Jesus loves us and forgives us—and that we will live in heaven with Him forever—is called the good news because it's. . .well, good! Jesus gives us victory and power to live good lives. And that's good too!

Who can you share the sweet news of Jesus with today?

Father, show me someone today who needs to hear about Jesus, and give me the words to share the good news. Amen.

DAY 60

LOVE OTHERS

Love does not give up. Love is kind. Love is not jealous. Love does not put itself up as being important. Love has no pride. Love does not do the wrong thing. Love never thinks of itself. Love does not get angry. Love does not remember the suffering that comes from being hurt by someone.

1 CORINTHIANS 13:4–5

The Bible says to love one another, right? But have you ever wondered exactly what that means? You have tender feelings for your mom and dad. . .because they're your family. But how are you supposed to feel that way about everyone, even people you don't know or don't like very much?

You can love everyone because God's kind of love isn't just a feeling—it's more of an action. It's something you do. A way of treating people.

The Bible says that you love others by being kind, having patience, doing the right thing, thinking of other people first, and forgiving others.

So you don't need to have gushy feelings to love like Jesus. Just choose to treat other people the way He did.

God, sometimes showing love is hard. Help me to choose love today. Amen.

DAY 61

NEVER GIVE UP

Let us not become weary in doing good, for at the proper time we will reap a harvest if we do not give up.
GALATIANS 6:9 NIV

Sometimes it seems like people who are doing the wrong thing get all the attention. You might be keeping your room clean, doing your homework, finishing your chores—all with a smile—but no one seems to notice. The mean girls at school are more popular and the selfish kids have all the stuff.

Don't give up! Don't stop doing the right thing. God sees everything you do. He notices even if no one else does. And He has awesome rewards waiting for the people who do what He says is right and good.

Even if it seems like bad behavior will get you what you want, the Bible says that those who do wrong will not have a good end. Remember that and keep on working for God. . .even when it feels like you want to give up.

Lord, help me not to get tired of choosing to do the right thing. I know You have a great reward waiting for me. Amen.

DAY 62

THE ANTIDOTE FOR FEAR

There is no fear in love. Perfect love puts fear out of our hearts. People have fear when they are afraid of being punished.
1 John 4:18

Do you ever worry that God might be mad at you? Maybe you did something you know you shouldn't have done. Or you feel as though God must disapprove of you for being too selfish or too silly. You feel as though you deserve to be punished and you keep expecting something bad to happen in your life.

But that's not the way God works. God loves you just the way you are. Of course God wants to help you grow and learn—but only because He longs for you to be all that He created you to be. God's love for you is so big that nothing you could ever do or not do would ever make it any less.

So open your heart to God's love. As you begin to realize that God's love for you is huge and real, you won't worry anymore about being punished. You'll know you're completely, totally, forever safe, surrounded by love.

Dear God, help me to believe in Your love. Thank You for loving me so much.

DAY 63

FALSE PREACHERS

My children, you are a part of God's family. You have stood against these false preachers and had power over them. You had power over them because the One Who lives in you is stronger than the one who is in the world.

1 John 4:4

The "false preachers" in this verse aren't people standing behind church pulpits shouting lies. The Greek word John used here when he wrote this Bible passage thousands of years ago means "spirit," "breath," or "wind." He was talking about people's ideas and even our own thoughts that twist or hide the truth of God's love. In other words, your own mind can be a "false preacher" sometimes! It can tell you that you're unlovable, that you're stupid, that you're ugly—and those are all lies.

God loves you so much that Jesus came to show you God's love in person. Jesus made you part of His family, and He sent His own Spirit—the Spirit of love and truth—to live inside you. You don't have to believe the lies that say you don't deserve to be loved. Instead, stand up straight and strong, knowing Jesus loves you immensely.

Jesus, make me strong in Your love.

DAY 64

STRONGHEARTED

"Be strong and have strength of heart. Do not be afraid or shake with fear because of them. For the Lord your God is the One Who goes with you. He will be faithful to you. He will not leave you alone."

DEUTERONOMY 31:6

Some people get nervous before a big exam or when they have to stand in front of the class to give an oral report. Other people are terrified of dogs or spiders or snakes. Going to the dentist or getting a shot is pretty scary for a lot of us, and you might be surprised to know how many people, including grown-ups, feel shy and uncomfortable when they meet new people.

Regardless of what frightens *you*, you don't have to face it alone. Whether it's a big exam, a big spider, a big needle, or a big crowd of people, God is *bigger*—and God is always right there with you. He will never abandon you. You can trust Him to take care of you, no matter what. His love will make you strong enough to face even the scariest things.

Thank You, God, that You will help me face the things that scare me. Thank You that Your love makes my heart strong and brave.

DAY 65

MAKING GOD VISIBLE

No person has ever seen God at any time. If we love each other, God lives in us. His love is made perfect in us.
1 John 4:12

When people look at you, do they see God? That may seem impossible—or maybe it seems vain or stuck up. But it's not. The Bible says that God is love, and that means whenever we truly love each other, God is there. God uses our love to show His love.

Back in the sixteenth century, a woman named Teresa of Ávila wrote these words about this same idea: "Christ has no body but yours, no hands, no feet on earth but yours. Yours are the eyes with which He looks compassionately on this world, yours are the feet with which He walks to do good, yours are the hands with which He blesses all the world. Christ has no body now but yours."

When you act in love, the people around you will see God.

Jesus, help me to be Your hands, Your feet, Your eyes. Use me to show Your love to everyone I meet today.

DAY 66

HE HOLDS YOUR HAND

"Do not fear, for I am with you. Do not be afraid, for I am your God. I will give you strength, and for sure I will help you. Yes, I will hold you up with My right hand that is right and good."
ISAIAH 41:10

Life can be scary. Not only do we hear on the news about bad things happening pretty much every day, but we also have to face hard things in our own lives. Friendships fall apart. People get angry with us. We make mistakes. Sometimes it all just seems so *hard*.

When you feel overwhelmed by life's hard things, try this—picture God walking beside you, holding your hand. If you trip, His hand will catch you and keep you from falling on your face. When you feel weak, He will give you His strength. And when you're scared, He'll whisper, "Do not fear, for I am with you."

God is better than any imaginary friend, because He's *real*.

I am so grateful, God, for Your presence in my life. Help me to feel Your hand in mine whenever I am scared.

DAY 67

TESTS

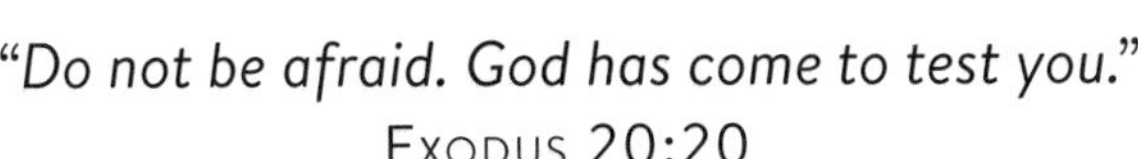

"Do not be afraid. God has come to test you."
Exodus 20:20

How do you feel about tests? Some people don't mind them, some people actually enjoy them, and some people hate them. However we feel about tests, they're usually just a fact of life when we're in school.

This Bible verse isn't saying that God will give us a spelling quiz or a final exam. It's talking about a different type of test. Both the English word and the Hebrew word in the verse come from a word for a pot where metal was heated and melted. Once it was melted, people could tell what the metal was made from. Was it pure gold? Or was it brass? The tests God sends us are like that. They're difficult things that help us see what's really inside us. We might find out that our faith in God needs to grow stronger.

God doesn't promise that He'll never send hard things into our lives. But we don't need to be scared of His tests, because no matter how good or bad we do, He'll never ever give us a big fat red zero or an F. Because He loves us so much, He just wants to help us grow.

God, show me what's inside me.
Test me and help me to grow.

DAY 68

SUPERPOWERS

We know that our life in this world is His life lived in us.
1 JOHN 4:17

Jesus wants to live His life through you. Can you imagine that? Your ordinary life—going to school, talking with your friends, doing your chores, eating dinner with your family, posting on Facebook, falling asleep—can be God's life. It's like having superpowers.

This means that you can share Jesus' relationship with the Father. You can talk to God the way Jesus did, knowing that God is always listening and loving. As Jesus lives His life in you, your life will start to have what the Bible calls the "fruit of the Spirit"—love, joy, peace, patience, kindness, gentleness, faithfulness, goodness, and self-control. You'll start to see these traits in all the things you do and say every day. They may not seem like superpowers, but they really are!

With Jesus living His life through you and in you, you'll be a supergirl.

Jesus, come live Your life in me. Give me Your superpowers. Make me the girl You want me to be.

DAY 69

IT'S SIMPLE!

Dear friends, let us love each other, because love comes from God. Those who love are God's children and they know God. Those who do not love do not know God because God is love.

1 John 4:7–8

Do you ever feel as though being a Christian is awfully hard? That there are too many rules, too many things to remember to do and not do? Grown-ups sometimes make being a Christian sound a lot harder than it really is. But the Bible makes it really simple.

It all boils down to love.

God wants you to love your friends, your family, your teachers, and even the people you don't really like all that much. He wants you to treat all of them with kindness—the way you want them to treat you. When you act like this, you are acting like God's child. And you'll be getting to know God better and better.

And if you don't act in love, when you're rude or mean to your friends, your family, your teachers, and all the people you don't like—well, then you can't really know God.

God, I want to know You better. Show me how to love all the people in my life. I want to be Your child.

DAY 70

FIGHTING THE BATTLE

"Today you are going into battle against those who hate you. Do not let your hearts become weak. Do not be afraid."
DEUTERONOMY 20:3

Do you ever feel like people hate you? They probably don't *actually* hate you, but sometimes people can be pretty mean. Even worse, though, is how mean we can be to our own selves.

If there's a part of you that doesn't like yourself very much—that maybe even hates yourself a little—you're not alone. Even grown-ups feel that way sometimes. There's a little voice inside us that says, *You're not good enough. You're not pretty enough. You're not smart enough*. Listening to that nasty little voice can make us weak when God wants us to be strong. It can make us shy and embarrassed.

But we don't have to believe the lies that hateful voice says. Instead, with God's help, we can do battle against it. Bad thoughts about yourself never come from God, so when you catch yourself thinking, *I'm ugly, I'm stupid, I'm bad*, ask God to help you. Read your Bible—and listen to God's voice instead.

That lying little voice is your enemy. Don't let it win.

God, help me fight the battle against the part of me that hates myself. Make me strong in Your love.

DAY 71

THE FEAR OF THE LORD

"Be very careful what you do. For the Lord our God will have nothing to do with what is not right and good."
2 Chronicles 19:7

Are you careful about what you do? Or do you not think about God very much throughout the day? Maybe you only think about Him on Sundays.

But if you're being mean to someone at school, stealing money out of your parent's wallet, or cheating on a test, God sees what you're doing. He's not waiting to catch you doing something bad so He can punish you, though. He's watching you because He loves you.

And He wants you to love Him back. When you really love God, you try not to do anything that would hurt someone. You're careful to do the things that show God's love to others. You remember that everything you do and say is important to God. You may feel as though you're small and unimportant sometimes—but what you do truly matters.

Dear God, remind me to be careful about what I do and say. I want to show You how much I love You—and I want You to use me to show others how much You love them too.

DAY 72

MAN'S WORDS

"Do not fear the shame of strong words from man. Do not be troubled when they speak against you."
ISAIAH 51:7

When the Bible uses the word *man*, it usually means "humans," not just male grown-ups. But sometimes, as girls, we can find male voices especially scary. Men can be bigger, louder, and stronger than girls.

Girls and women have a lot more rights than they did even a hundred years ago. We can vote and own property and have jobs that we enjoy. But even now, some men aren't very nice to girls. Sometimes they say things that make us feel embarrassed or ashamed.

God doesn't want you to be scared of anyone or anything, though. You don't ever need to be worried or embarrassed because of something someone says. God is always, always on your side, no matter what—and He will make you strong!

I'm so glad, God, that I can trust You to always listen to me, always take care of me, and always love me. You make me strong.

DAY 73

THE KING OF CONFUSION

"'Do not be afraid of the king of Babylon, who now fills you with fear. Do not be afraid of him,' says the Lord. 'For I am with you to save you and take you from his hands.'"

JEREMIAH 42:11

You probably haven't run into any scary kings lately. Most of the kings we hear about these days are in books or movies. But before you skip over this Bible verse, take another look. "Babylon" was an actual city in Bible times, but it was also a word that means "confused and mixed up." So we could say that "the king of Babylon" is someone or something that makes you feel mixed up and confused. Maybe it's math class. . .or trying to understand your parents when they're in bad moods. . .or why certain kids act the way they do. Maybe your own feelings make you feel confused. All of us have times when everything seems mixed up—and that can be scary.

But God doesn't want you to be afraid. It's okay to feel confused sometimes, but when you feel mixed up, remember—God will save you. He'll make everything clear again.

Thank You, God, that You will save me from the king of confusion. I'm counting on You.

DAY 74

THE SPIRIT OF POWER AND LOVE

For God did not give us a spirit of fear. He gave us a spirit of power and of love and of a good mind.
2 Timothy 1:7

There are plenty of scary things in the world. Even grown-ups get afraid sometimes. They read the news, and they wonder how things will ever work out. When bad things happen, all of us tend to feel afraid.

But God wants to make you strong and brave and full of love. He wants to give you His spirit of love. When the Bible was written, the word translated as "spirit" could also mean "breath." So the next time you feel afraid, try imagining that God is breathing on you. His breath is warm and gentle and full of love. Take a moment to breathe in. . .breathe out. . .and know that God's breath is inside you. You don't have to be scared anymore.

God, breathe on me, I pray.
Fill me with Your breath, Your Spirit.

DAY 75

DISAPPOINTMENTS

"My plans are torn apart, even the wishes of my heart."
Job 17:11

Don't you hate it when things don't turn out the way you hope? Maybe you've been looking forward to your friend's birthday party—but you get sick with a stomachache and can't go. Or you were hoping there was a new bike in the big box under the Christmas tree, but it turns out to be something boring you don't really want at all. Or maybe you were thinking you'd get picked to be in the school play, and one of your friends gets the part instead. It's upsetting when our wishes don't come true.

And it can be frustrating when we make plans that don't work out. Maybe you and your best friend plan a sleepover—but your parents say no. Or you come up with a great plan for a fun project—but you don't have the materials you need.

Life can be disappointing and frustrating. But God is with you through it all. He understands how you feel. He doesn't promise us that He'll make things turn out exactly the way we want—but He does promise that He'll always love us and never leave us.

When I feel disappointed, God, remind me that You are still there with me. Instead of getting mad, I want to trust You more.

DAY 76

GOD HAS PLANS FOR YOU!

"'For I know the plans I have for you,' says the Lord,
'plans for well-being and not for trouble,
to give you a future and a hope.'"
JEREMIAH 29:11

Do you ever wonder if God is like a really big, really grouchy grown-up, sitting up in heaven just waiting to say "*No!*" to everything you want to do? Especially when things don't turn out the way we hope, it can be easy to get mad at God and blame Him. But this Bible verse tells us that God has good things planned for us. Maybe it's nothing we've ever imagined. Instead, it's *better* than anything we could even dream.

God is planning right now all the ways He'll bless you throughout your life. Even when sad times come, that's not the end of the story. There's always something good, a blessing from God, waiting up ahead.

Thank You, God, that You love me so much. Even when life seems hard and sad, help me to trust Your plans for my life.

DAY 77

THE LORD'S PLANS

The plans of the Lord stand forever. The plans of His heart stand through the future of all people.
PSALM 33:11

Our plans don't always work out. It doesn't matter whether we're young or old, there are some things we just can't control. We plan to have a picnic, but it rains all day. We plan to make a batch of really delicious cookies, but they turn out hard and crumbly. We plan to get to school early, but we miss the school bus and end up being late. Those sorts of things happen to everyone sometimes.

But God's plans are different. He planned to send Jesus to show us how much He loves us—and He did. He planned for you to be born—and you were. He's planning right now to bless you in all kinds of amazing ways every day of your life—and He will!

I don't know what You have planned for my life, God. But I know You love me, so I'm going to trust You. I can't wait to see what You have in mind.

DAY 78

GOOD ADVICE

Plans go wrong without talking together, but they will go well when many wise [people] talk about what to do.
PROVERBS 15:22

Sometimes there are good reasons our plans don't work out the way we hope. Let's say you plan to make a gift for your grandmother, but then you don't have all the materials you need. Or you plan to get a good grade on a spelling test, but you study the wrong words. Maybe you plan to meet a friend after school, but you find out your parents have made other plans for you.

Things like this can be disappointing and frustrating. They can make you feel angry and discouraged. But if you had told your parents about the gift you wanted to make, they could have helped you get the materials you needed. If you'd checked with your teacher or with someone else in your class, you wouldn't have studied the wrong spelling list. And if you'd discussed your after-school plans with your parents ahead of time, they might have changed their own plans. When you take time to talk things over with other people, things usually go better!

God, thank You for all the people in my life. When I'm making plans, remind me to talk to them and get their advice.

DAY 79

TRUST

Trust your work to the Lord, and your plans will work out well.
PROVERBS 16:3

Trust is a word we see and hear a lot when we read the Bible or go to church. It's one of those words that we think we understand—but do we really? How would you explain what it means to "trust"?

Back when this part of the Bible was written thousands of years ago, the word used in this verse actually meant "roll away" or "roll onto," and the word for "work" had to do with something you do or make. So what this verse is saying is "Take everything you do and make, and roll it over to God." Whatever it is you're doing or making—and everything you plan to do and make—if you let it roll out of your hands and into God's hands, the end result will turn out better!

God, show me how to trust You. Teach me to let all my actions and all my plans roll into Your hands.

DAY 80

DON'T BE SELFISH

Do not always be thinking about your own plans only.
Be happy to know what other people are doing.
PHILIPPIANS 2:4

It's good to have a healthy self-concept. God wants you to like the person He created you to be. He wants you to enjoy being you. But He doesn't want you to act as though you are the center of the world. Instead, you're a part of a huge network of people and things. The choices you make and the things you do touch others.

So when you make plans for the weekend, check to see what your parents are doing. Don't just expect them to drive you wherever you want to go; they may have had an extra-tiring workweek, or they may need to run errands. Or if you're planning to have a birthday party, check to see what day would work best for your friends. Don't expect others to drop their own plans and do whatever you want!

Help me to remember, God, that I'm not the center of the world. You are!

DAY 81

YOUR HEART'S DESIRE

Be happy in the Lord. And He will give you the desires of your heart.
Psalm 37:4

Does it ever seem as though God doesn't want you to have the things you want? Do you ever wonder if God says no to everything that's fun, to all the things you really want to do?

God *does* want us to choose Him first, ahead of everything else. But when we do that, trusting Him to know what's best for us, being happy with whatever He sends into our lives, then He blesses us. He loves to give us things that will make us even happier.

Your heart is the deepest part of you, that secret part at the very center of you, the part that no one but God can see. And God made your heart. He's the one who put your deepest longings in your heart. So if, for example, you love animals, you can trust Him to bring animals into your life. Or if you love to draw, He will give you chances to learn more about art. If music is something you love, God will give you opportunities to be involved with music.

Put God first—and He'll give you the desires of your heart.

Thank You, God, for making my heart.

DAY 82

KEEP ON KEEPING ON

Those who keep on doing good and are looking for His greatness and honor will receive life that lasts forever.
ROMANS 2:7

Do you ever wonder what it means to be a Christian? Maybe there was a time when you decided you wanted to ask Jesus into your heart. And that was wonderful—but sometimes you wonder if it "stuck." You wonder if you're *really* going to go to heaven. You don't have to wonder. You never have to earn God's love. It's a gift He gives you for free, and He'll keep you safe in both life and death.

But being a Christian is something we do by following Jesus every day. Day after day, we follow in His footsteps, acting the way He wants us to. That means being kind to others. It means saying we're sorry when we make mistakes or hurt someone's feelings. It means talking to God and listening for His voice in our hearts. It means reading the Bible and learning more about God, and it means saying thank You to God all day, every day.

When we live like this, we'll stop wondering—and we'll know that God's love will carry us all the way to heaven.

I'm going to keep on keeping on, God, all the way to heaven.

DAY 83

RUN TO WIN!

Everyone who runs in a race does many things so his body will be strong. He does it to get a crown that will soon be worth nothing, but we work for a crown that will last forever. In the same way, I run straight for the place at the end of the race. I fight to win.
1 CORINTHIANS 9:25–26

Most things in life take practice. If you were going to run in a race, you would practice ahead of time. At first, you might not be able to run very far without getting tired and out of breath. But if you run every day, you'll get stronger and stronger, and after a while, you'll be running farther and farther. The more you practice, the easier the race will be for you.

Following Jesus is a little like that. At first, you make mistakes. You get tired of trying to do the right thing. You act selfishly and you want to be the center of the world. But then you say you're sorry and you try again the next day. And the next day. And little by little, living for Jesus gets a little easier. You get stronger.

You're running a hard race. Following Jesus is never going to be easy. But with God's help, you'll be a strong girl who runs straight toward Jesus every day.

Dear Jesus, I'm running for You. Put Your Spirit in me so I can be a little stronger every day.

DAY 84

THE ROCK THAT NEVER MOVES

"Do not fear. Do not be afraid. Have I not made it known to you from long ago? And you have heard Me. Is there a God besides Me? No, there is no other Rock."

Isaiah 44:8

Life is full of changes. Every year you are a little older and a little taller. That means you can do new things, but it can also mean you have to give up doing some things. You might have more chores or more homework than you did when you were younger. Your parents and teachers expect more from you. And then there are other changes that are bigger and harder. Your friends might move away and go to different schools. Or maybe your own family moves to a new house in a different part of the country. Someone you love might get sick or even die.

Change can be scary. It can make us sad. But God tells us we don't have to be afraid. Even when everything around us seems to be changing, He never does. His love for us is like a rock that will never move. We can stand on that rock and be safe—no matter how many other things change.

**God, I'm so glad You never change.
Be my rock, the safe place that will never go away.**

DAY 85
STRONG IN GOD

When I am afraid, I will trust in You.
Psalm 56:3

Here again we see that word *trust*. The word used in the Bible means "to run for safety." So when you're afraid, this verse is saying you should run to God, where you'll be safe. But how do we run to someone we can't see or touch? What does it really mean to run to God?

One way you could run to God is by taking some time to pray. If you're at school and you're feeling scared about something, maybe you could ask to go to the bathroom so that you can be alone for just a few moments to talk to God. Or you could talk to Him inside your head, without ever leaving your desk. You could run to God by leaving some time before you go to bed to read your Bible. Sometimes it might mean talking to a friend or grown-up you trust. Just as God uses you to show His love to others, He also uses the people in your life to show you His love.

Whatever way you find to run to God, one thing is certain—He'll always be there waiting for you!

When I am afraid, God, remind me to run to You.

DAY 86

GOD IS ALWAYS LISTENING

Answer me when I call, O my God Who is right and good! You have made a way for me when I needed help. Be kind to me, and hear my prayer.

PSALM 4:1

Have you ever tried to talk to someone who wasn't listening to you? Maybe they pretended to be listening, but you could tell they weren't really paying attention. Or maybe they didn't even bother to pretend. All the while you were trying to tell them something that was important to you, they kept looking at their phone or staring off into space.

When that happens, it hurts. But it never happens with God. When you talk to Him, He's always listening. He hears you when you call to Him. He wants to help you.

All you have to do is ask!

God, thank You for always listening to me. I need Your help today.

DAY 87

CARS AND COMPUTERS AND PHONES

Some trust in wagons and some in horses.
But we will trust in the name of the Lord, our God.
Psalm 20:7

Back when the Bible was written, wagons and horses were really important. Nowadays, not many people depend on wagons and horses to get them around. Instead, we have cars and computers and smartphones. But we're not really so different from the people who lived during Bible days.

Whether it's a horse or a car, a wagon or a computer, we depend on these things to make our lives easier. If your family has a fast and shiny new car or computer, you might feel proud that your family has more money—but if your family rides around in a car with lots of dents, or your computer is so slow that it takes forever for the internet to load, or you don't have a phone of your own, you may feel embarrassed.

But this scripture is a good reminder. Don't brag about your family's car or your computer or phone. Those things don't really matter very much. Instead, brag about God.

I'm going to trust only You, God!

DAY 88

NO REASON TO BE SCARED

The Lord is my light and the One Who saves me. Whom should I fear? The Lord is the strength of my life. Of whom should I be afraid?
Psalm 27:1

What makes people strong? Is it money? Is it an attractive physical appearance? Is it a closet full of nice clothes? Or a new phone and a new computer? Does having lots of friends make a person strong? Do strong people get good grades in school?

No—none of those things can make someone truly strong. Only God can make you strong. He's the only one who can shine His light into your life and heart. He keeps you safe. He gives you courage, and He never leaves you.

When I'm scared, Lord, remind me that You are with me. When I feel weak, remind me to lean on You. When I don't know which way to go, shine Your light to show me the right way. Make me strong in You.

DAY 89

SAFE AND FREE

O Lord, in You I have found a safe place.
Let me never be ashamed. Set me free.
Psalm 31:1

Do you ever feel ashamed? It's not a nice feeling, is it? It's kind of a squirmy feeling. You wish you could wriggle right out of your own skin and run away where no one can see you.

Different things make us ashamed—but even though it's a yucky feeling, sometimes feeling ashamed is a good thing. If we hurt someone or if we tell a lie or take something that's not ours, feeling ashamed can help us do the right thing by saying we're sorry, telling the truth, or making things right in some other way.

But other times, we might feel ashamed because someone did something wrong to us. We feel as though it were our fault. We feel as though we're small and weak and dirty. That's a really awful way to feel. If you ever feel like that, talk to a grown-up you trust. And talk to God.

No matter what we've done—or what someone else has done to us—God wants to set us free from those yucky feelings. We no longer have to be ashamed.

Set me free, God, from all the bad memories that make me feel ashamed. I pray this in the name of Jesus, my friend and Savior.

DAY 90

FIND OUT FOR YOURSELF!

O taste and see that the Lord is good.
PSALM 34:8

Remember the old book about green eggs and ham? The only way the funny creature found out how good green eggs and ham tasted was by trying them for himself. Knowing God is a little like that. You have to taste and see for yourself.

Going to Sunday school and church can be a good way to learn more about God. The teachers and the minister can teach you new things about Jesus. But that's not enough. God doesn't want you to just depend on what others say about Him. He wants you to find out for yourself just how wonderful He is.

So when it comes to God's goodness, don't take anyone else's word for it. Taste His blessings for yourself by praying and reading His Word in the Bible. See how good He is by paying attention every day, noticing all the good things He's doing in your life. Taste and see for yourself.

Dear God, show me how good You taste!
Help me to see how wonderful You really are!

DAY 91

GIVE IT TO GOD

Give your way over to the Lord.
Trust in Him also. And He will do it.
Psalm 37:5

Suppose you wake up in the morning, feeling excited about the day ahead. You're planning on all sorts of fun things happening. In fact, you're so excited that you never give God a thought.

But then things don't turn out quite like you'd hoped. You feel disappointed. You might even feel angry. You might be mad at God. After all, didn't He promise to help you? So what happened?

Let's pretend we can rewind this day and start over. This time when you wake up feeling excited, the first thing you do is pray, "Dear God, I'm excited about today. But first let me give it to You. I know You know what's best for me. Work everything out. I want Your way for my life." And this time, when things turn out a little differently from what you'd planned, you're able to see that God is doing something else, something even better. Even if you can't understand what He's doing, you know you can trust Him. You gave your way to Him, and that makes all the difference.

God, take my life. Even when I don't understand why things happen the way they do, I trust You.

DAY 92

STRAIGHT PATHS

Trust in the Lord with all your heart, and do not trust in your own understanding. Agree with Him in all your ways, and He will make your paths straight.
PROVERBS 3:5–6

Do you know someone courageous? What is that person like? Is she a know-it-all who charges out and insists on her own way? Or does she follow God and let Him lead the way?

People who are truly courageous—from the inside out—don't usually depend on their own strength to face the things they fear. No matter how smart they are, they know that God knows better than they do, and they give everything to God. Then, no matter how mixed up life can seem, they have the courage to walk straight along the paths God shows them.

Lord, help me to trust You more. I don't want to depend on my own smarts anymore. Whatever You want for my life, I'm ready to agree with You. Show me a path that will lead me straight to You.

DAY 93

BACKWARD AND FORWARD

For You are my hope, O Lord God.
You are my trust since I was young.
PSALM 71:5

This verse looks forward, toward the future—and sees God waiting there. "For You are my hope, O Lord God." And this verse looks backward and sees God also in the past. "You are my trust since I was young."

God was with you when you were a baby. He was there with you when you were a little kid. He's still here with you now that you're getting older. And He will be with you when you're a teenager, and then when you're an adult. He's never going to leave you.

When you look back at the past and see that God was there, even in the sad times and the hard times, it's a little easier to trust God with whatever is happening right now in your life. And it will give you courage to face whatever the future holds.

Thank You, God, that You've always been with me. You're with me right now, and You will be with me in the future. No matter what happens to me, You're always there with me.

DAY 94

SELFISHNESS

"You trusted in your sin and said, 'No one sees me.' Your wisdom and learning have led you the wrong way, for you have said in your heart, 'I am, and there is no one besides me.'"

Isaiah 47:10

Have you ever done something wrong that you kept a secret? Did you feel that if no one ever found out, then what you did wouldn't really matter? Most of us have probably had moments like that. *It didn't hurt anyone,* we tell ourselves. *And if no one knows what I did, then I'll never get in trouble. So what difference does it make?*

But when we do wrong, it does make a difference. Through God, all of us are connected to each other. That means even wrong things that seem small and unimportant can hurt others. And those ugly little secrets hurt God.

Don't trust yourself to hide those secrets away where they won't hurt anyone. Instead, take them to God. Ask Him what He wants you to do.

God, I don't want to talk to You about some of the things I do. This is hard for me—but I know You will help me. Give me the courage I need to do what's right.

DAY 95

RIGHT AND GOOD

The work of being right and good will give peace.
From the right and good work will come quiet trust forever.
Isaiah 32:17

God loves us no matter what we do. We don't need to earn His love by being good. So why bother to do what's right and good? Why not just do whatever we feel like doing?

Pay attention to what the verse at the top of the page is really saying. It's not saying that we should do what's right and good to make God happy. It doesn't say that if we want to go to heaven we have to be good. No, it says that doing what's right and good will give our own hearts peace. It will help us to trust God more.

Here's another way you could read this verse (using different words for the same thoughts): "Be fair to others and you'll be whole and strong (not broken and weak). Be kind and you'll feel calm and quiet and safe—forever."

God, I want to do Your work. Help me to be fair and kind. Help me to do what's right.

DAY 96

DON'T BELIEVE LIES!

"See, you are trusting in lies which cannot help you."
JEREMIAH 7:8

Lies are all around us—but maybe you don't notice them.

- You need to be pretty to be worthy of love.
- You need to be thin to be pretty.
- You need to be popular to be okay.
- You need to be "nice" and never speak out for what's fair.

All those things are lies. They're in television shows and movies. They're online and in magazines and in music. But here's the truth:

- God loves you no matter what you look like.
- God wants you to be healthy. He made your body perfect, just the way it is!
- God loves you and thinks you're wonderful, no matter what other people think of you.
- God wants you to speak up for what's right.

Help me, God, to trust You more.

DAY 97

QUESTIONS

You are right and good, O Lord, when I complain to You about my trouble. Yet I would like to talk with You about what is fair. Why does the way of the sinful go well? Why do all those who cannot be trusted have it so easy?

JEREMIAH 12:1

Did you know that it's okay to ask God questions? It's even okay to yell at God! People in the Bible did it all the time. Jeremiah, the man who spoke the words at the top of the page, was so close to God that he knew he could say to God, "What are You doing here, Lord? You promised me You'd bless me, but instead, it looks like You're blessing the people who do wrong things. What's going on?"

God answers Jeremiah. God says that He never promised that if we ignore Him and refuse to follow Him, He'll still bless us in the ways we want. We may have to deal with the consequences of our actions. But God isn't angry with Jeremiah for asking the questions. And He promises that as soon as His people turn back to Him, He'll bless them once again.

Dear God, I'm not sure what You're doing in my life. Sometimes I even get mad at You. Show me if I need to change what I'm doing. Bring me back where I belong.

DAY 98

GOSSIP

"You are happy when people act and talk in a bad way to you and make it very hard for you and tell bad things and lies about you because you trust in Me."
MATTHEW 5:11

Have you ever found out your friends were talking about you behind your back? Or have you ever felt picked on, either by other kids at school or by other members of your family? Maybe someone has said you did something bad that you never did. All those things can make life seem hard. They hurt.

But in this Bible verse, Jesus is saying that we can be *happy* when those things happen. Happy? Does that make any sense?

Well, no, it doesn't make any sense for people who don't know Jesus. But if you know Jesus, then you don't need to let these things bother you. What God thinks and does will matter to you far more than what other people say and do. You can rest in God's love, no matter what other people are saying and doing.

Jesus, it hurts when people tell lies about me and pick on me. So bring me closer to You. Help me to feel Your love and presence—and then I won't care so much what others say and do.

DAY 99

SPIRITUAL FOOD AND DRINK

Jesus said to them, "I am the Bread of Life.
He who comes to Me will never be hungry.
He who puts his trust in Me will never be thirsty."
JOHN 6:35

When Jesus said these words, the people around him were confused. These were people who had gone hungry sometimes. They didn't have a lot of money, and that meant they didn't always have enough food and drink. They followed Jesus so they could hear what He had to say to them, but now they felt mixed up. How could a person be bread? How could He promise they'd never be hungry or thirsty again?

But Jesus wasn't talking about stomach-hungry, and He didn't mean the kind of thirsty you get when you need a drink of water. He was talking about a different kind of hunger and thirst. He meant that there's a deep, deep part of you that cries out for love. . .the part of you that is hungry for meaning and purpose. "*I hear you,*" Jesus says, "*and you don't have to be lonely ever again. I understand you. I'm always paying attention to you. I'll never leave you.*"

Jesus, thank You for loving me so much!

DAY 100

GOOD MORNING!

Let me hear Your loving-kindness in the morning, for I trust in You. Teach me the way I should go for I lift up my soul to You.

PSALM 143:8

When you open your eyes, what's the first thought that enters your head? Maybe you're thinking about the day ahead—or maybe you're thinking about yesterday. Maybe those thoughts make you happy, but maybe they make you feel scared or sad. Maybe you wake up knowing that you just have to hurry off to school, and you don't have time to even *know* what you're thinking.

But the man who wrote the verse at the top of the page knew a different way to wake up. As soon as he woke up, he said hello to God. He took a moment to remember that God loved him. He asked God to show him the way to go that day.

You can do the same.

Dear Lord, help me to start each day right. Remind me to say "Good morning" to You.

DAY 101

LIVING WATER

"Rivers of living water will flow from the heart of the one who puts his trust in Me."
JOHN 7:38

Jesus said these words to the people who were following Him. Another time He said He was the "Bread of Life," and now here He is talking about "living water." What do you think He meant?

The verse that follows this one (John 7:39) says that Jesus was talking about the Holy Spirit. Why do you think Jesus would say that the Holy Spirit was like living water? Maybe because we can't live without water. Without water, we would die. And we need the Spirit of God to live just as much as our bodies need water.

Notice that in this Bible verse Jesus isn't saying that rivers of living water—the Spirit—will flow out of *Him*. Instead, He's saying that the Spirit will flow out of anyone who trusts Him. That means *you* can be like a faucet—and the water of God's Spirit will flow through you out into the world.

Jesus, help me to trust You more. I want the water of Your Spirit to flow through me. Use me to bless others. May my life show them Your love.

DAY 102

LIGHT

"I came to the world to be a Light. Anyone who puts his trust in Me will not be in darkness."
JOHN 12:46

Jesus said a lot of things about Himself that can seem confusing. He said He was like bread and like water. And here He's saying He is like light. He's saying that He came into the world to be a light. What do you think He meant?

Imagine what our world would have been like if Jesus had never come! Without Him, we wouldn't know as much about God. We wouldn't be able to understand who God is as well as we do now. We would probably feel more confused and be more unhappy and scared.

But Jesus *did* come. He came to show us God. He came so we would know how much God loves us. He came so we wouldn't feel so mixed up and sad and scared. He came to shine light into our darkness.

Jesus, when I'm mixed up and sad, please shine Your light into my life and into my heart.

DAY 103

TRUST JESUS

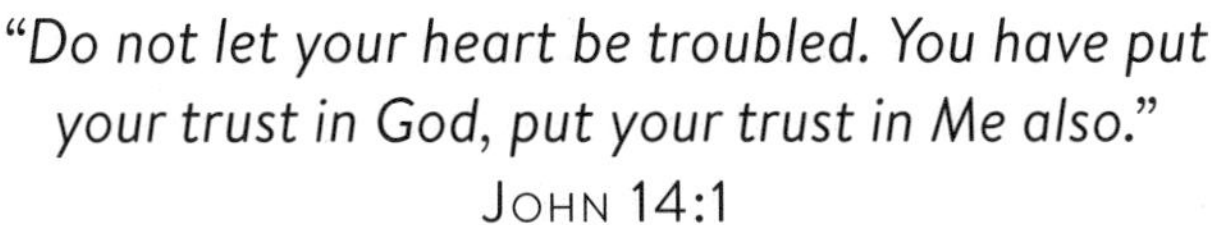

"Do not let your heart be troubled. You have put your trust in God, put your trust in Me also."
JOHN 14:1

Jesus was the Son of God—but He was also a human being just like you and me. He had hands and feet, shoulders and knees, fingernails and toenails. He had to go to the bathroom. He got sad and happy, angry and excited. He loved His friends. He is still alive, still real, and He loves you.

"God" is a huge idea. God is so big that we can never wrap our heads around who God is. But Jesus came to earth to show us God in a way we can understand. He came to show us God with hands and feet (and fingernails and toenails). And then He died for us, to show us just how very much God loves us.

So when someone loves you that much, why be scared of anything? You can trust someone who loves you so much that He lived and died for you.

Jesus, help me to trust You more. Make me courageous.

DAY 104

TRAPPED

We have become free like a bird out of a trap.
The net is broken and now we are free.
Psalm 124:7

The Bible often compares our lives and God to other things. It does this to help us understand God better. It uses something we do understand to help us understand something that's hard to understand. This verse is talking about traps—but it doesn't mean the sort of trap you might put out to catch a mouse. It's talking about anything that keeps you from growing into the person God wants you to be.

Traps come in all shapes and sizes. A trap might be a bad habit you have that you can't seem to stop. A trap could be a friendship that isn't good for you. Or a trap could be a sickness. . .or feeling so shy that you're scared to talk to people. . .or a situation you don't know how to handle.

Whatever trap has caught you, God can help you escape. He is always on your side—and since He is the one who made heaven and earth, He has the power to set you free.

God, when I feel trapped,
remind me that You can set me free.

DAY 105

ANGER

Shake with anger and do not sin. When you are on your bed, look into your hearts and be quiet.
Psalm 4:4

When the Bible uses the word *sin*, it's the same word that was used to talk about an arrow that didn't hit the target. Getting mad is not a sin—but anything that controls us, other than the Spirit of God, can throw us off target. It can make us lose track of where God wants us to go. We might have a good reason to be mad—but if we hold on to our anger, it can build a wall between us and other people, and between us and God too.

The man who wrote this Bible verse so many years ago has good advice for us. He says: "Think about things overnight before you say anything. Rather than saying something in the heat of the moment, think carefully about how God wants you to act. Calm down. Search your heart to see if you're partly to blame. Ask for God's help."

God, it's hard to remember You when I'm mad. The next time I'm angry, please remind me to turn to You. Remind me to be quiet and listen to what You have to say to my heart.

DAY 106

GOOD FRUIT

But the fruit that comes from having the Holy Spirit in our lives is: love, joy, peace, not giving up, being kind, being good, having faith.
GALATIANS 5:22

Don't beat yourself up if you feel selfish sometimes. Everyone does. Being selfish is just part of being human. That selfish side of us always wants its own way, so it gets angry when it doesn't get it. That in turn can lead to all sorts of other problems—fights, hurt feelings, misunderstandings, and broken friendships. But if we're following Jesus, we've decided to give up our selfishness. We're following Jesus and living in a new way.

No one says this is easy. It's not. But when you let God's Spirit fill you, you won't have to work so hard at being a nicer person. The closer you are to God (the more time you spend with Him), the more your life will just naturally produce a new sort of fruit—love, joy, peace, courage, kindness, and goodness.

Jesus, I want to hang all my selfishness on Your cross. Give me the courage to follow You so that Your Spirit can produce sweet fruit in my life.

DAY 107

WORRIES

Do not worry. Learn to pray about everything.
Give thanks to God as you ask Him for what you need.
PHILIPPIANS 4:6

When we worry, we're imagining something that *might* happen—even though it might *never* happen. We picture all the terrible things that *could* happen. We let worry eat up all our thoughts until we're so scared, we can't think about anything else.

But this scripture tells us it doesn't have to be like that. Instead, you can turn your worries into prayers. When you talk to God about the things that worry you, Jesus will come into that worried place inside you and fill it with His peace and love. He will show you new ideas for dealing with all the things that scare you. He will help you, and He will give you courage.

Help me, Jesus. You know how worried I feel, but I want to give this worry to you. Every time it pokes me, making me feel scared all over again, remind me that You have everything under control.

DAY 108

ARGUMENTS

Let me say it again. Have nothing to do with foolish talk and those who want to argue. It can only lead to trouble.
2 Timothy 2:23

When something is wrong, God wants you to have courage and speak up. He might want you to take action to put things right. But the verse at the top of the page isn't talking about that kind of thing. This verse is talking about getting into fights just because you want to be right. When you argue to prove how smart you are or that you're better in some other way, you're not putting things right. Instead, you're making trouble.

Some arguments are about silly things. If you took a moment to actually listen to the other person, you might find there is no reason to argue at all. God wants you to be patient and kind. He wants you to be willing to listen to other people, even when you think they're wrong. If you really listen, you'll understand the other person better—and you'll be able to avoid trouble!

God, show me when I should be quiet and listen. Help me not to get into silly arguments.

DAY 109

NOTHING'S IMPOSSIBLE!

God is able to do much more than we ask or think through His power working in us.
Ephesians 3:20

Imagine every good thing that God has promised in the Bible, all the things we've talked about so far. Now think of the things you daydream about, the wonderful things you wish would happen. Remember all of the prayers you've brought to God. And now read again the verse at the top of the page.

God can do even more than you can imagine. He's not a magic genie who will answer all your wishes of course. Instead, He is doing something even bigger than all your wishes, bigger than all the prayers you've ever prayed. He's doing things that seem impossible. His power has no limits.

So don't be afraid to pray for big things.

God, I know You can do things that seem impossible. Show me how You want me to pray. Help me to follow Your lead, even when it seems like You're doing something impossible.

DAY 110

YOU BELONG!

"All whom My Father has given to Me will come to Me. I will never turn away anyone who comes to Me."
JOHN 6:37

You belong to Jesus. The Father called your name—and when you heard that call and came to Jesus, He held out His arms to you. "Welcome home," He said to you. "I'm so glad you're here. I want to help you. I will save you and keep you. I'll give you courage and make you strong. I love you so very much. Tell me everything that's important to you. No matter what happens, I'll never leave you."

People let us down. Parents, friends, everyone—sooner or later, they all hurt us and disappoint us. No matter how much they love us, they're only human. They make mistakes. They fail to understand us. But Jesus will always understand you. He'll never disappoint you. He'll never ever let you down.

Jesus, I'm so glad You are my friend. I want to get to know You better. Help me, I pray. Show me how to follow You. Thank You that You and I belong together.

DAY 111

THE LORD OF SHINING-GREATNESS

Our Lord Jesus Christ is the Lord of shining-greatness. Since your trust is in Him, do not look on one person as more important than another.

James 2:1

Jesus shines. He is the food your spirit longs for. He satisfies all your longings. And He is the light that shines on your life. Whenever you are discouraged, whenever you're lonely, whenever you're mixed up, whenever you're sad, He is waiting to shine His light into your heart.

But we get mixed up so easily. We can't *see* Jesus, so we start focusing on the people in our lives. We think their ideas and opinions are more important than what Jesus thinks. We feel good about ourselves—or bad about ourselves—based on the opinions of others, when all along the only thing that matters is what Jesus thinks.

Jesus, You are the Lord of shining-greatness. Shine Your light, I pray, into my life. By Your light, may I see more clearly. Help me not to care so much about what other people think. Show me what is truly important—and what is not.

DAY 112

NO MORE TEARS

"God will take away all their tears.
There will be no more death or sorrow or crying
or pain. All the old things have passed away."
REVELATION 21:4

We all cry sometimes. Friends hurt our feelings. Beloved pets die. Our parents scold us. Things don't turn out the way we hope. Tears are a part of all our lives.

But this Bible verse describes a different kind of life, one that none of us have yet known. In that life, the life that Jesus has planned for each one of us, we'll be able to see God. We'll talk face-to-face with Jesus. We'll finally know, really and truly, how much He loves us. We won't need to cry anymore about anything.

It kind of sounds too good to be true, doesn't it? But God understands why we might find these words hard to believe—so He told John, the man who wrote this verse, to write, "See! I am making all things new. Write, for these words are true and faithful" (Revelation 21:5).

Every tear you cry now will be wiped away in heaven.

Jesus, thank You that You're making a new home for me in heaven, a home where I'll never need to cry again.

DAY 113

THE POWER OF LOVE

If I have the gift of speaking God's Word and if I understand all secrets, but do not have love, I am nothing. If I know all things and if I have the gift of faith so I can move mountains, but do not have love, I am nothing.

1 Corinthians 13:2

The Bible makes it clear that one thing is more important than anything else. It's not reading your Bible, going to church, obeying all the rules your parents and teachers give you, or making people think you're strong and important and good. All those things can be good, but the Bible says one thing is more important—*love*. That's the one word that says what it means to follow Jesus. It's the one word that describes God.

The kind of love the Bible is talking about isn't really a feeling at all. What it comes down to is what's sometimes called the Golden Rule—"Treat others the way you want to be treated." Be kind. Be considerate. Be gentle. Be patient. Those are the things that really matter. Those are the things that will bring you closer to God. And those are the things that will let God use you to show His love to everyone you meet.

**God, show me how to love.
Use me to love everyone in my life.**

DAY 114

POWER!

I thank God I can be free through Jesus Christ our Lord! Now, because of this, those who belong to Christ will not suffer the punishment of sin. The power of the Holy Spirit has made me free from the power of sin and death. This power is mine because I belong to Christ Jesus.

Romans 7:25–8:2

We all feel guilty about some of the things we've done. Sometimes we make mistakes, even though we truly meant to do something good. Other times we hurt others because we're being selfish and we're putting ourselves first, ahead of God and other people. Even Christians still make both kinds of mistakes.

Guilt is feeling bad because we've done something wrong. When that happens, we need to say we're sorry and ask God to show us how to make things right.

God is making you into a new person. He is making you into a strong and courageous girl. He is making you more like Jesus.

Jesus, forgive me for my mistakes—for all the times I've messed up and all the times I've been selfish. Show me how to be more like You. Free me from my sin. Make me powerful in Your love.

DAY 115

BELIEVE WITHOUT SEEING

You have never seen Him but you love Him. You cannot see Him now but you are putting your trust in Him. And you have joy so great that words cannot tell about it.
1 PETER 1:8

Sometimes it's hard to follow a person you've never seen. If your friends don't believe in Jesus, you may feel a little silly trying to explain what He means to you. You might even feel as though He's like an imaginary friend, and you could feel embarrassed to talk about Him. But Jesus is not make-believe. He's *real*. He lived and breathed and walked on the earth—and now He is with God in heaven.

We don't understand what heaven is. It could be another dimension, another world that's invisible to us in this world. But we don't need to understand heaven to know that Jesus is alive, that He loves us, that He is with us. And when we trust Him, when we believe that He will take care of us and show us the way to live our lives, then we can share His joy and love.

Jesus, I've never seen You, but I love You. Help me get to know You better, even though I can't see You. Help me to trust You more.

DAY 116

JESUS PRAYED FOR YOU!

"I do not pray for these followers only.
I pray for those who will put their trust in Me
through the teaching they have heard."
John 17:20

Jesus prayed for each one of us. He prayed for me—and He prayed for you. Can you imagine that? When Jesus was here on earth, He prayed for you! You were in His mind, and He prayed that you would be strong and whole. He knew how hard your life would be, and He asked His Father to help you.

When you feel weak or small or discouraged, remember that Jesus prayed for you. He loved you before you were even born, and He loves you today. You are precious to Him, and He wants to help you.

Jesus, thank You for praying for me. Help me to trust You more and more. I am so glad that You love me.

DAY 117

FEELING DISAPPOINTED?

God is not a man, that He should lie. He is not a son of man, that He should be sorry for what He has said. Has He said, and will He not do it? Has He spoken, and will He not keep His Word?
NUMBERS 23:19

We all feel disappointed sometimes. People let us down; they promise they'll do something—and then they don't. Things we hope will happen don't. But God promises that He will never disappoint us. When He makes a promise, He always keeps it. He doesn't lie or exaggerate. So when He says He'll bless us, He will!

The next time you're feeling disappointed, take a moment to think about your life. Are you trusting God—or are you thinking that other people should make you happy? Everyone, no matter how much they love you, will let you down sooner or later—but God never will. If you're depending on Him, you'll never be disappointed.

Teach me, Lord, to rely only on Your promises. Thank You that You never break Your word. Remind me not to depend on people—and help me to forgive people when they let me down.

DAY 118

DOUBTS

Jesus said to them, "Why are you afraid? Why do you have doubts in your hearts?"
LUKE 24:38

Do you ever wonder if God is *really* real? Almost everyone does. Believe it or not, doubt is normal. And it's not a sin to doubt. But doubt that continues for a long time can cause us pain. It can rob us of the peace and joy God wants us to have. It can get in the way of us growing into the people God wants us to be.

You'd think that Jesus' friends, who had seen Jesus work miracle after miracle, would no longer doubt Him. That wasn't the case, though. Like all human beings, they could be filled with faith and love one minute, and then be scared and doubting the next. And yet Jesus did not scold them for their doubt. Instead, He came to them, talked to them, and showed them Himself.

He longs to do the same with you. When doubts overcome you, He says, "*Don't be scared. I'm here. I'm real. You can believe in me. I won't let you down.*"

Jesus, please show me Yourself. Use even my worries and doubts to draw me closer to You.

DAY 119

TRUTH

Wash me inside and out from my wrong-doing and make me clean from my sin. For I know my wrong-doing, and my sin is always in front of me. . . . See, You want truth deep within the heart. And You will make me know wisdom in the hidden part. Take away my sin, and I will be clean. Wash me, and I will be whiter than snow. . . . Hide Your face from my sins. And take away all my wrong-doing. Make a clean heart in me, O God. Give me a new spirit that will not be moved. Do not throw me away from where You are. And do not take Your Holy Spirit from me. Let the joy of Your saving power return to me. And give me a willing spirit to obey you.

Psalm 51:2–3, 6–7, 9–12

Lies and mean words can slip from our mouths so easily. But the person who wrote this Bible passage knew that truth is important to God. We need to be honest with ourselves and God. How can we be close to God—or anyone else—if we're lying to ourselves and others?

The first step to a close friendship with God is to admit our lies and ask God's forgiveness. God can wash away everything untruthful and mean in our hearts.

Spirit of God, give me Your power, please. Make me clean. Help me to obey You.

DAY 120

JEALOUSY

When you are jealous and fight with each other, you are still living in sin and acting like sinful men in the world.
1 Corinthians 3:3

What makes you jealous? Maybe you feel jealous when a friend seems to like someone else better than you. Or maybe you're jealous when you think your parents are paying more attention to your brother or sister.

Jealousy hurts. It makes us feel as though we're not good enough. It can make us act mean and hurt others around us. But this Bible verse says we don't need to feel this way any longer. God loves us so much that there's no reason for us to be jealous. God has given us everything we need to be happy.

God, help me to pay more attention to You so that there's no room in my life for jealousy. Remind me that You have given me everything I need. Give me the courage I need to live for You.

DAY 121

A TREE IN GOD'S HOUSE

I am like a green olive tree in the house of God.
I trust in the loving-kindness of God forever and ever.
PSALM 52:8

What does it mean to be a tree in the house of God? Well, a tree is strong. It has deep roots that draw up water from the earth. And a tree grows tall. It has wide branches where birds and other animals can live. So if you are like a tree, that means you too are strong. God gives you what you need to grow and grow, year after year. He makes you so strong and courageous that you can help others. He makes you tall and beautiful and full of life. Trees don't have to worry about life. They simply stand in one place, trusting in God's goodness.

Dear Lord, help me to trust in Your kindness. Make me like a tall green tree. Use me to shelter and help others. Make me beautiful and strong.

DAY 122

IT'S ALL ABOUT LOVE

We have come to know and believe the love God has for us. God is love. If you live in love, you live by the help of God and God lives in you.
1 John 4:16

This Bible verse spells out very clearly what it means to follow Jesus. It all comes down to love. So when being a Christian seems too hard and complicated, reread this Bible verse.

God loves you. And God wants to use you to spread His love out into the world. He wants to use your hands, your mouth, your mind, your ideas, your eyes, your feet, your everything to put more and more love out into the world.

If you live in love, you live in God—and God lives in you. Imagine that!

God, show me how to love. Make me courageous and strong. Put Your love in me so that everyone I see and everyone I speak to can sense Your love flowing through me. Thank You for loving me!

DAY 123

COURAGE TO BELIEVE

They said, "Put your trust in the Lord Jesus Christ and you and your family will be saved from the punishment of sin."
ACTS 16:31

It's not always easy to believe in God, especially when friends make fun of you for your faith. They might ask questions like, "Where is your God? I can't see Him." You can't see Him either, but you've seen Him work in your life. He's healed sick people you know, taken care of your family when you were going through a hard time, and even helped you with your schoolwork.

God wants to give you courage to go on believing, even when it's really hard. So if you're going through a hard time right now, have courage! Keep believing, even if it doesn't make sense. If the doctors are saying, "She won't get well this time," keep praying, keep believing.

Thanks for giving me courage to believe, even when things seem impossible, Lord! Amen.

DAY 124

JESUS TEACHES ABOUT THE CARES OF LIFE

"I tell you this: Do not worry about your life. Do not worry about what you are going to eat and drink. Do not worry about what you are going to wear. Is not life more important than food? Is not the body more important than clothes?"
MATTHEW 6:25

Are you a worrier? Do you lie in bed at night with too much on your mind? Maybe you're worried about that big test you have to take. Or maybe you can't stop thinking about that girl in school who always picks on you.

Truth is, there's a lot you could worry about if you let your mind go there. But Jesus wants you to know that you don't have to worry about anything, even the big stuff. Why? Because He has it all under control. He knows how to provide for you, to give you everything you need and more.

Do you trust Him? If so, don't worry!

Sometimes I get really worried, Lord. But then You calm me down and remind me that I can trust in You. Amen.

DAY 125

TRUST. . . NO MATTER WHAT

Trust in the Lord with all your heart,
and do not trust in your own understanding.
PROVERBS 3:5

When you flip the switch to turn on the lights, do you trust that the lights will come on? When your dad puts the key in the car, does he have faith to believe the car will start? When your mom mixes up eggs, butter, sugar, and flour, does she trust she can bake a delicious cake?

To trust means you truly believe something will happen. You have no doubts, even when things don't seem to be going your way. You just keep hoping and believing.

The Bible says you can put your trust in God. The words you read in His Word (the Bible) are 100 percent true. If He said it, He will do it. You can trust Him with every problem you face. Don't try to figure it out on your own. Just have faith that God will take care of things.

Even when my situation seems impossible, Lord, I will trust You. Amen.

DAY 126

FOCUS ON OTHERS

Do not always be thinking about your own plans only. Be happy to know what other people are doing.
PHILIPPIANS 2:4

If you're like most girls, you get really excited about your plans—that party you're looking forward to, that visit to your grandparents' house to celebrate Christmas, your upcoming birthday party. You can't wait for any of it. If you had your way, it would all happen right now.

It's fun to have something to look forward to, but it's just as important to care about the other people in your life—your friends, your parents, your neighbors, the people you know at church, even your teacher and principal. What are they looking forward to? What plans are they making for the future? Have you taken the time to ask?

Maybe it's time to take your eyes off of your own adventures and spend some time getting excited with your friends about their plans.

It's not always easy to put others first. Sometimes I forget and think only of myself. Thanks, Lord, for giving me the courage to put others' needs before my own. Amen.

DAY 127

WITNESS

You are the light of the world.
You cannot hide a city that is on a mountain.
MATTHEW 5:14

Imagine it's almost bedtime—it's dark outside. Suddenly, without warning, all the lights in the house go out. No electricity! You know there's a flashlight in the closet, but how can you get there in the dark? You pinch your eyes shut and then open them, hoping it will help you see better. No such luck!

Somehow, you make your way to the closet. You open it, stumble around, and finally find the flashlight. When you snap it on—*bam*!—light fills the room. You shine that light and it shows you where to walk safely.

The Bible says you are the light of the world. You're like that flashlight. When you shine brightly, people know where to walk safely.

Are you shining bright today? Have courage to step out!

Sometimes I'm scared to let my light shine
because I'm afraid people will make fun of me.
But You give me courage, Lord! Amen.

DAY 128

YOU WON'T QUIT!

I have fought a good fight. I have finished the work I was to do. I have kept the faith.
2 TIMOTHY 4:7

Maybe you know what it's like to give up. You're studying for a big test, but you don't feel like it. So, you quit studying and play a video game. Then you wonder why your grade on the test isn't the best. Or maybe your mom tells you to clean your room. You start, but you don't finish. You get distracted looking at an old toy.

Sometimes it's easy to get distracted, isn't it? But the Lord wants you to keep going, even when you don't feel like it. (That's true courage!)

Finishing what you start is so important, especially when it comes to your walk with God. You can't say, "Sure, Jesus! I'll follow You!" and then give up. He wants you to keep your faith in Him always, not just when you feel like it.

Jesus wants you to finish what you start. So get busy!

**I won't give up on You, Jesus.
I'm so glad you never give up on me. Amen.**

DAY 129

USING YOUR GIFTS

For this reason, I ask you to keep using the gift God gave you. It came to you when I laid my hands on you and prayed that God would use you.
2 Timothy 1:6

Imagine it's Christmas morning. You open your presents under the tree. One of them is an amazing bike you've been hoping to get. You can't believe it! You want to ride it right away, of course. No one can get you off of it.

Then, after a few weeks, you get bored with it. You stop riding it. Months later, you see that it has a flat tire. You don't really care because you don't ride it anyway. Then a couple of years later, you notice there are cobwebs all over it. Wow! You really should clean that bike up and actually use it, shouldn't you?

The same is true of the gifts God has given you. Whether you sing, act, dance, or memorize scripture for the Bible quiz, He wants every single gift to be used for Him, not just now, but for years to come.

What are some God-given gifts you need to start using again?

Lord, I'm ready to start using all of my gifts for You. Give me the courage, I pray. Amen.

DAY 130

PRACTICALLY PERFECT IN EVERY WAY?

O Lord, who may live in Your tent? Who may live on Your holy hill? He who walks without blame and does what is right and good, and speaks the truth in his heart.

Psalm 15:1–2

Maybe you read this verse and think, *Does God expect me to be perfect? I'm not even close!* No, the Lord doesn't expect perfection from you, but He does want to remind you that doing your best, making good choices, is the best way to stick close to Him.

What kind of choices, you ask? Well, how you treat others, for example. How you talk to your mom. How you respond when your teacher gives a big assignment.

Making good choices in other areas of your life is important too—working hard, being kind to all people, making others feel included, and so on.

Do any areas of your life need improvement? Do the right thing and deal with them right away.

Lord, I'm definitely not perfect, but I'm trying! Help me make good choices, I pray. Amen.

DAY 131

ALL THINGS

I can do all things because Christ gives me the strength.
PHILIPPIANS 4:13

Repeat these two words out loud: all things. Say them again: all things.

Today's verse says that you can do all things through Christ who gives you strength. When you're facing a hard test in school and you think you won't make it, He will give you strength. When you need to work up the courage to talk to that girl who's been making fun of you, God will strengthen you.

Why do you suppose the Lord wants you to know that it's His strength, not yours? If you had to depend on yourself, you would panic. Even the strongest human being is weak compared to God. So depend on His strength. Let Him do what you can't do. When you step aside and let God work, He really can do *all* things.

I'm glad it's Your strength, not mine, Lord. I'm pretty weak compared to You. I'm like a weight lifter when I allow You to do the work through me. Amen.

DAY 132

THE FUTURE

"'For I know the plans I have for you,' says the Lord, 'plans for well-being and not for trouble, to give you a future and a hope.'"
JEREMIAH 29:11

God knows the future. Think about that for a minute. You don't have any idea what's going to happen five minutes from now, or even an hour from now. Anything could happen! It's out of your control.

But God knows. He can see into the future, all the way to the part where you're going to be in heaven with Him. He knows how old you'll get, how many children you'll have, what sort of job you'll have when you grow up. . .everything!

He has great plans for you, girl. You can't see them yet, but He can. And God has a very active imagination, so you can count on those plans being amazing!

Lord, it's exciting to think that You know what's coming next in my life. I don't know. . .but You do. Thank You for thinking up great plans for my life, Father! Amen.

DAY 133

A TRUE FRIEND

Two are better than one, because they have good pay for their work.
Ecclesiastes 4:9

Have you ever tried to move a really heavy piece of furniture by yourself, something like a piano or a big dresser? It's impossible, isn't it? But when a second person comes along—your dad, your big brother, a strong friend—together you get the job done.

That's how life is. So many projects are easier when you have someone working with you. This is one of the reasons God decided that marriage was a good idea. When a girl grows up, she's strong and ready to face whatever comes her way. But when she marries a godly man, together they're like a chain that can't be broken. They're super-duper strong.

Who are your strongest friends? Today, take the time to thank God for them. Then pray that your friendships will grow even stronger as you get older.

I'm so grateful for my friends, Lord! Together, we are very, very strong! We are like a chain that can't be broken. Amen.

DAY 134

COURAGE TO LOVE

"The second is like it, 'You must love your neighbor as you love yourself.'"
MATTHEW 22:39

God gave us a couple of big commands: to love Him most of all, and to love others as we love ourselves. If you've asked Jesus into your heart (you have, haven't you?), then loving Him most of all is easy. But loving others as you love yourself? That's a little trickier.

Sometimes we want things our own way. We don't like to put others' needs above our own.

Here's an example: Your school is doing a play. You're trying out for a big part and you really think you might get it. Your friend is talented too, and she's never had a big part before. You both audition for the same part. . .and you have a hard time feeling happy for her when she gets it.

God wants you to celebrate your friend's accomplishments and to wish her the very best, even if it means you don't get what you want. It's hard, but in the end you'll be so happy you loved her as much as you love yourself.

Help me to have the courage to love my friends Your way, God! I want the best for them. Amen.

DAY 135

NO PAYBACKS, GIRL!

When someone does something bad to you, do not do the same thing to him. When someone talks about you, do not talk about him. Instead, pray that good will come to him. You were called to do this so you might receive good things from God.
1 Peter 3:9

Oh, how you want to get even! That boy on the bus called you a terrible name and you're tempted to get in his face and call him a name or two. But you don't. You remember this verse from 1 Peter about praying for those who hurt you. *Ugh.* You don't want to pray for him. You'd rather get even.

God's not about getting even. He wants us to release our anger and pain to Him and to trust that He will take care of things in His own way and His own time. It's not easy. In fact, living this way is very, very hard at times and takes a lot of self-control. But the Lord will give you the ability to calm yourself, even when you're really mad.

No paybacks. No getting even. Just. . .love.

Father, this is a tough one! You saw what they did to me. You heard what they said! But I trust You to take care of it. You've got my back, Lord. Amen.

DAY 136

IF YOU LOVE . . .OBEY

"If you love Me, you will do what I say."
JOHN 14:15

Maybe you've heard Mom use these words: "If you love me, you won't talk to me like that!" Or maybe Dad has said, "If you love me, you'll do what I ask you to do."

"Loving" and "doing" go together like peanut butter and jelly. They're a great team. When you truly love someone, you want to please them. So you do what they say because you love to see them smile.

Making God smile is easy. Just obey His Word. Do what He says to do. Love others. Treat them as you would want to be treated. Don't let your temper get the best of you. Don't be selfish or rude. These are all areas where He's hoping you'll obey.

Do you love Him? Great! It's time to live an obedient life.

I do love You, Lord. In fact, I love You most of all! Because I love You, I will also obey You. I'll pay closer attention to what the Bible says and do my very best. Amen.

DAY 137

HOW CHILDREN MUST LIVE

Children, as Christians, obey your parents.
This is the right thing to do.
Ephesians 6:1

Have you ever wondered why God makes such a big deal out of children obeying their parents? Why does it matter?

Imagine *you* were the parent. You told your kids to clean their rooms, but they never did. You told them to eat their food, but they refused. You told them to take a bath, but they didn't feel like it. It wouldn't be long before your children were dirty, starving, and living in a pigpen!

Parents put rules in place for your own good. If you break those rules, the one who suffers is always you. It's better to obey.

The main reason God cares so much is because obeying your parents is a sign that you love them. When you do what they ask, you're proving (to God and others) how much you love them. When you love someone, you would do anything for them, so let that love flow, girl!

Lord, I get it! The rules are there to protect me.
I want my parents to know how much I love them.
Give me courage and determination to obey! Amen.

DAY 138

STOP THE GOSSIP TRAIN

I will stop whoever talks against his neighbor in secret. I will not listen to anyone who has a proud look and a proud heart.
PSALM 101:5

Gossip is like a train, isn't it? It moves down the track from one person to the next. Before long everyone knows the juicy story.

The problem with gossip is that it hurts people. Some people share half-truths—only part of the truth but not all of it. Some people spread lies. Some people make stuff up just to hurt someone they don't like. Others spread gossip to make a popular person look less popular.

Has anyone ever gossiped about you? It's a terrible feeling, knowing people are talking about you behind your back. God doesn't like it either. That's why He says in His Word that you have to stop talking in secret to your friends. And you must close your ears to gossip too. Don't listen to it anymore. Those who gossip just want to get you upset with the person they're upset with, after all.

Lord, please forgive me for the times I've gossiped. Help me to shut my mouth and not spread rumors. And close my ears to gossip too, Father. I want it gone from my life. Amen.

DAY 139

GOD, MY ROCK

The Lord is my rock, and my safe place, and the One Who takes me out of trouble. My God is my rock, in Whom I am safe. He is my safe-covering, my saving strength, and my strong tower.
PSALM 18:2

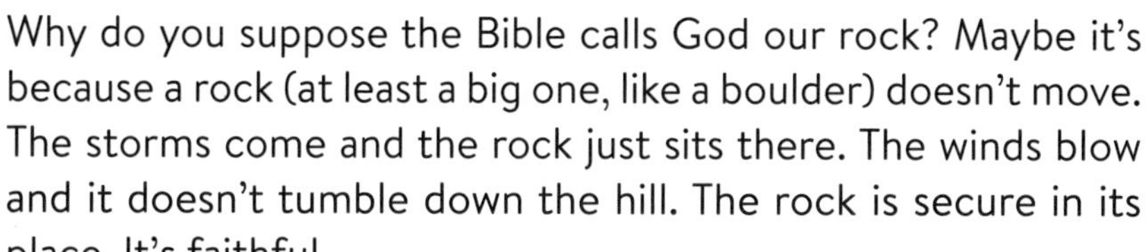

Why do you suppose the Bible calls God our rock? Maybe it's because a rock (at least a big one, like a boulder) doesn't move. The storms come and the rock just sits there. The winds blow and it doesn't tumble down the hill. The rock is secure in its place. It's faithful.

God doesn't move. He doesn't change. The words He spoke in the Bible are as true today as they were thousands of years ago. People all around you might disappear—some will move away, and others simply won't want to be friends anymore. But like that rock, God won't move. He's in your life to stay.

A rock is strong. God is the strongest of the strong. What no one else can do. . .He can do. He still performs miracles. God is our rock. You can count on Him no matter what!

Thank You for being my rock, Lord! I'm so glad You never move. I can always run to You when I lose my courage. Thank You for always being there. Amen.

DAY 140

HOW FORGIVENESS WORKS

If we tell Him our sins, He is faithful and we can depend on Him to forgive us of our sins. He will make our lives clean from all sin.
1 JOHN 1:9

Some people say, "God will forgive me no matter what." But they never ask for forgiveness. They don't even regret what they did. They just expect God to say, *"It's okay! No problem!"*

Is this how forgiveness works? Does God really just forgive everyone for everything, no matter what?

This verse explains how God decides whether or not to forgive something. If you confess your sin (you admit you did it and you're sorry you did it, not just sorry you got caught), He's faithful to forgive.

Today, take a look at your life, especially things you've done that you regret. Have you admitted them to God? Are you truly sorry? If so, then He will gladly forgive you for those sins and you never have to worry about them again. You can totally forget they ever happened. Whew! What a gracious God we serve!

Lord, I'm so sorry for the times I've messed up. Thank You for Your forgiveness. Amen.

DAY 141

WHAT'S ON YOUR MIND?

Christian brothers, keep your minds thinking about whatever is true, whatever is respected, whatever is right, whatever is pure, whatever can be loved, and whatever is well thought of. If there is anything good and worth giving thanks for, think about these things.

PHILIPPIANS 4:8

What are you thinking about right now? Maybe you're hungry and you're thinking about lunch. Perhaps you're worried about a friend who's mad at you. Maybe you're thinking about all the things you need to do before you go to bed.

No doubt your mind is busy, busy, busy—you're always thinking, thinking, thinking!

Did you know that God cares about your thoughts? He wants to make sure you're thinking about good, positive things. Don't worry about what you can't control. Don't spend time thinking about how mad you are at someone. Instead, think about how good God is, how forgiving and merciful. Think about His great love for you.

There! Don't you feel more courageous when You're thinking about Him?

Lord, I want to keep my thoughts on You!

DAY 142

WAIT. . .AND GET STRONGER

But they who wait upon the Lord will get new strength. They will rise up with wings like eagles. They will run and not get tired. They will walk and not become weak.

Isaiah 40:31

Most kids don't like to wait. They want what they want and they want it *now*. Today, if possible!

Would you consider yourself to be patient or impatient? If you knew you were going to be awarded a trophy at an upcoming school program, would you wait patiently until that day or would you wish, wish, wish it would happen right this minute?

Waiting is hard, but this scripture verse tells us that the people who wait on God get stronger and stronger. The longer you have to wait, the stronger you get. Wow!

When you think of it like that, then waiting is a good thing. God is teaching you things while you're waiting and growing you into a strong young lady.

While you're waiting, practice these words: "I'm getting stronger with time!" It's true, you know!

Thank You for reminding me that I'm getting stronger with time, Lord. I will do my best to wait with patience! Amen.

DAY 143

BE A JESUS COPYCAT

This is the way to know if you belong to Christ. The one who says he belongs to Christ should live the same kind of life Christ lived.
1 John 2:5–6

Have you ever played copycat? Maybe your friend said something and you repeated her words back to her. Or maybe she wore a pink shirt to school one day so you decided to wear pink the next.

Copycatting can be good or bad, depending on your heart. If you're making fun of the person, it's bad. But if you're copying their behaviors or manners out of respect, it's a good thing.

When it comes to Jesus, copying Him is *always* a good thing. You're saying, "I want to be like You, Lord!"

So how can you copycat Jesus? Let your words be words of love, just like His. Treat others with respect. Pray for people who are sick or in trouble. Don't judge them. Make things easier on others. That's how Jesus loved.

Today, make up your mind to copycat Him by living as He lived.

**Jesus, I want to be like You!
Show me how, every single day. Amen.**

DAY 144

KEEPING PROMISES

The Lord is not slow about keeping His promise as some people think. He is waiting for you. The Lord does not want any person to be punished forever. He wants all people to be sorry for their sins and turn from them.

2 PETER 3:9

Has anyone you know ever broken a promise? Maybe Dad promised to take you fishing on the weekend but he ended up working. Or maybe Mom said, "Sure, we'll go to the mall and look for new school clothes," but she forgot.

People let us down a lot. They usually don't do it on purpose. Friends promise to hang out with us but don't. Parents promise to spend time with us but have jobs to do. It's easy to get disappointed, isn't it?

Did you know there's someone who never breaks a promise? God is a promise keeper. If He said He's going to do something, He will do it. . .every single time.

God wants you to be a promise keeper too. Don't let people down. If you say you will do something, do it.

I want to be a promise keeper like You, Lord! Give me courage to do so, I pray. Amen.

DAY 145

STRONGER HOPE

Our hope comes from God. May He fill you with joy and peace because of your trust in Him. May your hope grow stronger by the power of the Holy Spirit.
ROMANS 15:13

Have you ever hoped for something, even if it didn't make sense? Maybe you knew your family couldn't afford it, but you hoped, hoped, hoped you could go to Disney World. Or maybe you knew you probably wouldn't get an A on the big test, but you hoped you would anyway.

Hope is a wonderful gift from God. It's not something you come up with on your own. Hope means you're trusting God. Hope brings peace. Hope brings joy. Hope keeps you from worry, worry, worrying all the time.

Did you know that your hope can grow? It's true! You know how your feet are always growing? You change shoe sizes all the time. Well, hope is like that. When you put your trust in Jesus, the size of your hope gets bigger, and bigger, and bigger!

Doesn't it feel good to have hope?

Thank You for giving me hope, Lord! I'm happy and at peace because I've placed my hope and trust in You. Amen.

DAY 146

TRUST HIM, NOT YOURSELF

Trust in the Lord with all your heart, and do not trust in your own understanding.

Proverbs 3:5

You think you have it all figured out. Then something happens and you realize you didn't have it figured out at all.

Has that ever happened to you? Maybe a friend got mad at you and you didn't know why. You thought about it and thought about it, and finally said, "I know! She must be mad at me because of something I said." Only you find out later she wasn't mad at you at all. Her family was going through a rough time after her dad lost his job.

God never intended for us to know everything. That's why He says we have to trust (have faith) in Him. We don't have it all figured out. . .but He does. And because He knows everything, He already has a plan to work things out.

You can trust Him, even when you don't understand.

Lord, I do trust You. I don't always get it. I don't know why things happen the way they do. But I know I can count on You. Give me the courage to do so. Amen.

DAY 147

LET'S ALL GET ALONG

See, how good and how pleasing it is for brothers to live together as one!
PSALM 133:1

Have you ever worked in the nursery at your church? Or maybe you've helped your mom take care of your younger brothers and sisters.

Whenever you put a lot of kids together in one space, they often begin to squabble and fight. Oh, not you of course. You would never do that. But some kids do.

Why do you think kids argue when they get together in groups? Because every single one wants his or her own way. When you get that many people all demanding their own way, things can get crazy in a hurry!

What if people stopped demanding their own way? What if everyone said, "That's okay. We can do it your way instead of my way"? Wow! People would start getting along for sure.

What about you? Do you squabble if you don't get your way? Maybe it's time to let go of a fighting attitude and get along with others.

Father, I want everyone to have a turn so that we can all get along.

DAY 148

BE A CHEERFUL GIVER

Each man should give as he has decided in his heart. He should not give, wishing he could keep it. Or he should not give if he feels he has to give. God loves a man who gives because he wants to give.
2 Corinthians 9:7

Why do you suppose God asks us to give cheerfully—to have a good attitude about giving?

It matters because He wants to bless us as we give. That can't happen if we have stingy thoughts, if we're clinging to our money or our possessions too much. But if we let go and give with a happy heart, we see that God is really blessing others through us. Every time that happens, we get blessed too!

Do you give to the Lord? Have you given an offering at church? Have you donated to a food pantry or given clothes to a family in need? The more you give, the happier you'll be. God loves a girl who loves to give.

I want to be a cheerful giver, Lord. Sometimes that takes courage! I don't want to hold too tightly to the things I care about. Please help me give from my heart. Amen.

DAY 149

DON'T ACT LIKE THE WORLD

Do not act like the sinful people of the world. Let God change your life. First of all, let Him give you a new mind. Then you will know what God wants you to do. And the things you do will be good and pleasing and perfect.
ROMANS 12:2

Some people just act crazy, don't they? They're disobedient to their parents, rude to their teachers, and mean to kids on the playground. It's like they think the rules don't matter.

The Bible says you should never act like those people. When God changes your life, He makes everything new, and that includes your thoughts. If you change your thoughts, if you start listening to God and reading your Bible, then your actions will change. You won't be like a lot of the other kids anymore. . .and that's a good thing.

You want to live in a way that is good and pleasing to the Lord. Give Him your heart and let Him change you from the inside out. Pretty soon the mean kids will be acting like you.

I want to be like You, not like the sinful people I know, Lord. Help me, please! Amen.

DAY 150

SHARP FRIENDS

Iron is made sharp with iron,
and one man is made sharp by a friend.
Proverbs 27:17

Friends make us better. Okay, sometimes they get on our nerves. They think they're funny when they're really not or they poke fun at us. But mostly they're a blast to be around.

All of that is great, but why do you suppose God says that friends make us sharper? Are we all supposed to walk around with pointy heads like pencils? Of course not!

Back in the old days, people would sharpen their knives or swords by rubbing them together—iron against iron. This Bible verse shows us that friendship is a lot like that. When we hang out with friends, they make us better and we make them better.

How do we do that? By loving them. By saying, "Great job!" after they've done something well. By hugging them when they are sad. By saying good things about them behind their backs.

Today, decide to be a "sharp" friend, one who blesses and encourages those you love.

I love my friends, Lord, especially the ones who keep me sharp. Give me courage to keep them sharp too. Amen.

DAY 151

GOOD THINGS ARE COMING

I am sure that our suffering now cannot be compared to the shining-greatness that He is going to give us.
ROMANS 8:18

Life is filled with ups and downs. Some days are amazing. Other days are rough. You wish you could skip the bad days and only have the good, but life isn't like that.

On the bad days, when you feel like giving up your courage, remember this: Jesus said that the bad stuff we're going through here on earth can't even begin to compare with the amazing things we're going to experience in heaven. There we won't have any rough days. We'll only have happy, carefree ones.

So if you're going through a hard time, look up! A day is coming when all of your suffering will be behind you. You'll spend eternity walking on streets of gold, singing with angel choirs and worshipping the one who loves you most of all.

Lord, thank You for reminding me that heaven is going to be great. I'm going through a lot of stuff here—and it's hard—but it will be worth it all in the end. Amen.

DAY 152

EVERYTHING

The Lord is my Shepherd. I will have everything I need.
PSALM 23:1

Think about the things you need to survive: food to eat, water to drink, a house to live in, money to pay the bills, people to help you.

Of course, you have a list of "wants" too: friends to do life with, a cool bedroom to call your own, electronics to play with, yummy snacks, outdoor fun, and maybe a pet dog or cat.

Take a look at today's verse. God says that He is your shepherd. (A shepherd takes amazing care of his sheep. He doesn't let the wolf come in and attack them!) The shepherd watches over his little lambs and makes sure they have food, water, and plenty of sunshine.

That's how God is with you. He knows what you need and makes sure you have it. Sometimes, just for fun, He gives you a few things from your wish list too.

Father, thank You for being such a good shepherd. I have all I need because I have You! Amen.

DAY 153

BE ON THE LOOKOUT

"I am sending you out like sheep with wolves all around you. Be wise like snakes and gentle like doves."
MATTHEW 10:16

Not everyone is a good guy. There are some people out there who want you to believe they're sweet but they're really not.

That's why you have to keep your eyes wide open! You have to be on the lookout for people who want to lie, steal, cheat, or hurt others.

Maybe you've seen kids like this at school. They seem okay at first, but when the teacher's back is turned they're using bad language, bullying other kids, or making fun of others behind their backs.

Today's verse says that God is sending you (His daughter) out as a sheep among wolves. That means you're going to have people all around you who are up to no good. But don't be scared! Use your God-given courage! You're a strong sheep because your shepherd (God) is protecting you. You have nothing to worry about. Just keep your eyes open and protect yourself and others from the wolves!

Help me keep my eyes wide open, Lord! I will stay away from those kids who are doing the wrong thing. Amen.

DAY 154

LOVE COMES FROM GOD

Dear friends, let us love each other, because love comes from God. Those who love are God's children and they know God.
1 JOHN 4:7

Do you love your family? Do you love your friends?

That love you feel when you're holding a tiny baby or having a fun conversation with a friend comes straight from God. He has filled your heart with love and it spills over onto others.

Loving others doesn't always come easy. Some people are hard to love. But because God has placed love in our hearts, there's always plenty to share.

How does the world know you're a Christian? (Have you ever thought about that?) They know because of how you love others—both the lovable and the unlovable.

Is the world seeing your love? Do you show it in the way you treat kids at school? Do you show it in the way you talk to your parents? Does it show in your conversations with your best friend?

Let love lead the way.

Love comes from You, God! I thank You for loving me and for showing me how to love others. Amen.

DAY 155

PRAY IN SECRET

"When you pray, go into a room by yourself. After you have shut the door, pray to your Father Who is in secret. Then your Father Who sees in secret will reward you."
MATTHEW 6:6

Why do you suppose Jesus told His disciples to go into a room by themselves to pray? What is so hush-hush about prayer?

For one thing, it's good to go to a quiet place to pray so that you're not distracted. There are no TVs, no loud music, no kids screaming. Getting alone with God means you can think more clearly. You can share your thoughts, your concerns, your love. You can listen to Him speak.

Did you realize that God speaks? He whispers thoughts into your mind, and He speaks through His Word too. When you're sitting in a quiet place, you can listen—really listen—for His still, small voice. He's saying things like, "*You've got this, girl!*"

When was the last time you went into a quiet, secret place to pray? Maybe right now is a good time.

**I love spending time with You, Lord.
I speak, You listen. You speak, I listen.
How great is that? Amen.**

DAY 156

WATCH YOUR TALK

Watch your talk! No bad words should be coming from your mouth. Say what is good. Your words should help others grow as Christians.

Ephesians 4:29

When the Bible says, "Watch your talk!" what do you think that means?

Sometimes we slip up and say mean things. We don't mean to, but the words come rolling out when we're angry.

Sometimes people say really bad things. They use bad language or they take God's name in vain. They don't even think about what they're saying. They just say whatever they feel like saying.

Words are like weapons. You need to choose them (and use them) very carefully. They have the power to hurt people.

Of course, words also have the power to bring joy to others and to lift their spirits. That's how God wants you to use your words. Instead of mean, negative things, speak life, hope, and joy to others.

No bad words for you, girl!

Lord, help me choose my words carefully. Help me bring life to others, I pray. Amen.

DAY 157

OBEY YOUR LEADERS

Obey the head leader of the country and all other leaders over you. This pleases the Lord.
1 Peter 2:13

What do you think of when you read the words, "Obey your leaders"?

Who are these leaders, anyway? Are they your teachers, your church leaders, the president of the country? Are they your parents, your grandparents, your aunts and uncles?

"Leaders" are people who lead you. Anyone who teaches or trains you would be considered a leader. Do your parents teach and train you? Of course! So do other relatives. Teachers teach, and so do church leaders. So when you think about it that way, you have a lot of leaders in your life. (If you ever want to play follow the leader, it might get confusing!)

God wants you to obey the leaders of your country, your church, and your home. When you do, you bring honor to Him and to all those you treat with respect.

I will obey my leaders, Lord. I will do what they say because I want to please Your heart. Amen.

DAY 158

WHO'S YOUR BOSS?

"No one can have two bosses. He will hate the one and love the other. Or he will listen to the one and work against the other. You cannot have both God and riches as your boss at the same time."
MATTHEW 6:24

Who is your boss? Your mom? Your teacher? Your grandfather?

That's an interesting question, isn't it? You are supposed to respect and obey the leaders in your life of course, but who is the real boss? Who makes the decisions? Who gets the last word?

The big boss is God. He created the world and knows how it should be run, so He's the one who gets to make the big decisions. Your dad asks God, "What kind of job should I have?" Your mom asks Him, "Can you help me figure out how to be a great parent?" Your grandmother goes to Him and asks, "Can I have a long life so that I can spend time with my grandchildren?"

Everyone goes to the big boss with the big questions, and you should too. If you lose your courage, instead of running to your friends, pray about it. If a friend is sick and you don't know what to do, talk to the big boss. He is hoping you'll come to Him.

You're the boss of me, God! I love having such a wonderful boss who cares so much. Amen.

DAY 159

IT'S ALL TRUE

Every word of God has been proven true.
He is a safe-covering to those who trust in Him.
PROVERBS 30:5

Imagine you're on the playground at school. Your friend is telling a story. It's pretty dramatic and after a while you start to wonder if all of it is true.

People sometimes exaggerate or make things up, but God never does. If you read something in His Word (the Bible), you can count on it being true. When He says (in John 3:16) that He loved the world so much that He sent His Son. . .it's true! When He says (in 1 John 2:25) that He offers eternal life. . .it's true! When He says (in Luke 18:27) that He can do impossible things. . .it's 100 percent true.

God wants you to know that you can trust Him. He's not going to make up any stories. And He actually follows through. He does what He says He will do. (He's a God of His word!)

Aren't you glad God is faithful and true?

God, I know I can trust You! You don't make things up. I can count on Your promises to come true. Amen.

DAY 160

MADE BY GOD

For You made the parts inside me.
You put me together inside my mother.
PSALM 139:13

Have you ever looked at a toy to see where it was made? Some are made in America. Some are made in other countries. Maybe you've looked on the backs of the plates in your cupboard and have seen a stamp saying "Made in China."

Where something is made is important, but so is *how* it is made. If the company uses cheap parts, the toy will break apart. If those china plates aren't real china, they aren't as valuable.

You were made by God. The same God who made elephants, zebras, rivers, and mountains made you. He knit you together in your mother's womb. That means, before anyone ever saw you, God was already working on you.

He made you just like you are and He's so proud of the way you're living. You were made to do amazing things and you're off to a great start.

Lord, I get it! I have an invisible "Made by God" stamp on my forehead. You created me in Your image and I'm so proud to be Your child. Amen.

DAY 161

HE KNOWS WHAT YOU'RE THINKING

Even before I speak a word, O Lord, You know it all.
Psalm 139:4

Have you ever wished you could read someone's mind? That you could tell what they're really thinking? Maybe you hurt your friend's feelings and you apologized. She says things are okay, but her face says, "I'm still mad at you." You wish you could tell what she was really thinking because you want her to forgive you.

Did you know that God can see inside your mind? He knows your every thought. He knows what you're going to say before you ever say it.

Whoa! That's crazy to think about, right? God knows when you're about to blow it by saying something mean, and He's whispering in your ear, "*Don't say that! Choose kinder words!*" He knows when you're angry or when someone has hurt your feelings. He knows when you need more courage.

Because God knows. . .He cares. Isn't it wonderful to think that your thoughts matter to God?

**God, I'm glad You can read my thoughts,
because You can help me choose my words.
Give me good words, I pray. Amen.**

DAY 162

ARE YOU LISTENING, LORD?

Listen to my cry for help, my King and my God. For I pray to you.
Psalm 5:2

Have you ever had a conversation with someone who didn't seem to be paying attention? Maybe later they forgot everything you told them. You probably wondered if they were listening at all. Maybe you just wasted your breath.

Some people feel like that when it comes to prayer. Because they can't see God, because they can't seem to hear His still, small voice, they wonder if He's even listening.

Today's verse shows us that we need to cry out to God for help, and to keep praying, even when we can't tell if He's listening. It's not always easy, but don't give up on praying, even if you don't get the answers you need.

God *is* listening. He has never stopped listening to you, not ever. He cares very much about the things that matter to you. So don't give up on Him. Just keep praying.

I'll keep praying, Lord. I won't quit. I trust that You hear me. Amen.

DAY 163

HE'S THE GREATEST

O Lord, our Lord, how great is Your name in all the earth. You have set Your shining-greatness above the heavens.
PSALM 8:1

How many great people are there in the world? Some people would say that kings and queens are great (and they are). Some would say that Hollywood stars are pretty great. (They certainly dress up like royalty sometimes.) The world is filled with "great people."

You know quite a few of them yourself, don't you? You might say, "My grandma's pretty great!" or "I love my teacher. She's great!" You might even say, "My mom is the greatest mom in the world" (and you really mean it).

It's true, there are a lot of "great" people in the world. But there is one who is greater than everyone else, and that's God. The Bible says His shining-greatness is above the heavens. Even the twinkling stars know His name. The trees and mountains bow when they hear the name of Jesus. Wow, all of nature knows how great He is!

Do you?

God, You're the greatest of the great. I worship You because of who You are! Amen.

DAY 164

GOD MADE GIRLS

The Lord God made woman from the bone which He had taken from the man. And He brought her to the man. The man said, "This is now bone of my bones, and flesh of my flesh. She will be called Woman, because she was taken out of Man."

Genesis 2:22–23

If you've read the book of Genesis, you know the story of Adam and Eve. Adam didn't have a helper or a friend, so God put Adam into a deep sleep, took out one of his ribs, and made a woman (Eve) out of it.

That's an amazing story! The very first woman on the planet came from a man's rib. Crazy-cool, right?

God has always felt that girls are special. He loves them just as much as He loves boys.

Never feel that you're not as good as someone else because you're a girl. God breathed His life into you and has given you courage to do great things for Him.

Watch out, world! This girl is ready to do some great things for God!

Thanks for making me a girl, Lord!
I'm ready to do great things for You. Amen.

DAY 165

TAKE COURAGE AND REST WITHOUT FEAR

And so my heart is glad. My soul is full of joy.
My body also will rest without fear.
Psalm 16:9

Do you know what it means to truly have courage? It means that you've placed your trust in God, not yourself. When you do that (even if you're going through a hard time), you can put your head on your pillow at night and rest.

Trusting Him means you can have a glad heart instead of worrying. It means that joy can take the place of sadness. When you truly trust Him, everything changes.

Stop trying to "get courageous." It's not something you can do on your own. It's not like a book you pick up off the table. God has to give it to you. If you want to rest easy and sleep well tonight, ask for God's courage. He'll give you the very best.

Lord, I want to sleep and be at peace, so I trust You to give me Your courage. Amen.

DAY 166

KEEP SPEAKING

Paul saw the Lord in a dream one night. He said to Paul, "Do not be afraid. Keep speaking. Do not close your mouth."
ACTS 18:9

Wow, what a dream Paul had! (Can you even imagine seeing God in a dream? That would be incredible!) The Lord told Paul not to be afraid. He also told him to keep speaking.

This dream tells us a lot about Paul. He was an amazing man who traveled all over—from city to city—telling people about Jesus. There were times when people didn't want to hear what he had to say. He was probably scared to keep sharing the good news. But Jesus told Him to be brave and not give up. When God said, "Do not close your mouth," He was saying, "Don't let your fear stop you. Keep on speaking, even when you're nervous."

Maybe you feel nervous when you're telling people about Jesus. That's okay. Just keep speaking and don't be afraid.

Thank You for giving me courage to speak up, Lord. Amen.

DAY 167

GOOD THOUGHTS

Let the words of my mouth and the thoughts of my heart be pleasing in Your eyes, O Lord, my Rock and the One Who saves me.
PSALM 19:14

It's so important to guard your words. They have the power to hurt people, if used incorrectly. But did you know it's also important to guard your thoughts? If you let your mind wander to things that are bad, then your actions will follow. Good thoughts = good actions.

It works like this: You're mad at a friend. You keep thinking and thinking about what she did to hurt you. She comes to you to apologize, but you're so stuck on what she did that you can't forgive her. You said, "No way! You're no friend to me."

See what happened there? Your thoughts became your words and actions. Because you couldn't stop thinking about what she did, she's no longer your friend.

God wants you to have good thoughts and good words and actions. He wants your thoughts to be pleasing to Him. Can you do it? Of course you can!

I'll do my best to have good thoughts, Lord! Please help me. Amen.

DAY 168

YOU CAN'T OUTGIVE GOD

"Give, and it will be given to you. You will have more than enough. It can be pushed down and shaken together and it will still run over as it is given to you. The way you give to others is the way you will receive in return."
LUKE 6:38

God's Word says that if you give, you will receive. Today's verse says that you'll get so much back in return that you won't have room for it.

Do you think God is only talking about money here? Probably not! Imagine you hear about a family in need. You and your mom go to the grocery store and buy food for them. Later that week, you get an unexpected blessing. Your grandparents show up at your house with a car that they no longer drive. They want to bless your family by giving it to you.

Wow! That's just one example of how the Lord blesses those who give. And remember, you can never outgive God. When you give, He always gives back.

I know I can never outgive You, Lord, but I want to try! Show me how I can bless people. Amen.

DAY 169

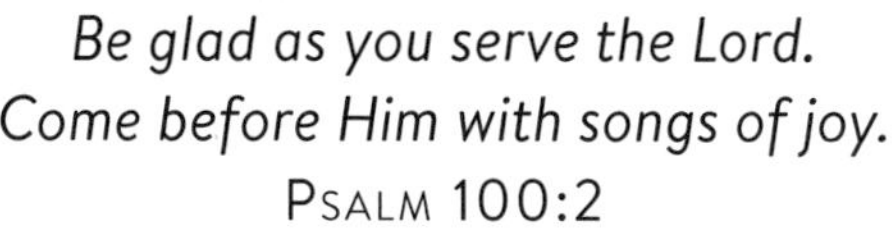

SONGS OF JOY

Be glad as you serve the Lord.
Come before Him with songs of joy.
PSALM 100:2

Are you one of those girls who always has a song in her heart? Does it feel like it's bubbling up from inside of you, destined to come out? Do you go around the house singing at the top of your lungs? Do you love singing worship songs at church? If so, then keep it up! God loves to hear His girls sing.

Christians have a lot to sing about. God has saved us, blessed us, given us wonderful families, and even helped us overcome obstacles like fear and pain. He's done so much for us, it's hard *not* to sing.

So don't hold back. Don't worry about what others think. Make a joyful noise to the Lord. Come before Him with songs of joy. The Lord loves for His kids to praise Him in this way.

Lord, today I praise You with a song. I want to praise You for all You've done for me and for the people I love. Thank You, Father! Amen.

DAY 170

IT'S NOT ABOUT STUFF

Keep your lives free from the love of money.
Be happy with what you have. God has said,
"I will never leave you or let you be alone."
HEBREWS 13:5

Some people just love their stuff. You can tell when you visit their homes. They have beautiful cars, expensive furniture, and all sorts of collectibles around the house, including expensive art on the walls. Their homes are like museums!

There's nothing wrong with beautiful stuff. In fact, it's fun to decorate your home and make it a place you love. But when stuff—electronics, bikes, clothes, and so on—becomes too important, watch out!

The Bible says we're to keep our lives free from the love of money (and the stuff it can buy). We're supposed to be happy with what we have.

What about you? Are you happy with what you have, or are you always begging for more? Don't forget, God will give you everything you need. And remember, there's a big difference between what you need and what you want.

I don't need a lot of stuff, Lord. I have everything I need and more already. Amen.

DAY 171

KINDNESS AND TRUTH

Do not let kindness and truth leave you. Tie them around your neck. Write them upon your heart. So you will find favor and good understanding in the eyes of God and man.

PROVERBS 3:3–4

This is an interesting verse. Do you think God really wants you to tie the words *kindness* and *truth* around your neck and write them on your heart? If not, what does He mean?

The Lord is telling you to keep these words close to your heart so that you never forget to treat others the way you want to be treated.

It matters to God that you treat others well, especially those who are being bullied or made fun of. It might take courage to go against the crowd, but when you do, amazing things happen. Other kids see and they learn from you. Before long, the bullies are feeling ashamed of how they've acted.

Be brave. Be kind. It's God's way.

Lord, I want to write these words on my heart so that I never forget to treat others with kindness and truth. Help me, I pray. Amen.

DAY 172

PLEASING OTHERS

Or if you do ask, you do not receive because your reasons for asking are wrong. You want these things only to please yourselves.

JAMES 4:3

Sometimes we ask for things just because we want them for ourselves. We're not thinking about what's best for those around us. God hopes that you'll ask for things that will be helpful to other people.

Example: Instead of begging your mom for that next video game, why not ask your friends, parents, and other loved ones to help you raise money to send to a missionary in Africa? Instead of demanding a new bike for Christmas, keep the old one and ask Mom to use that money on something for herself.

It's so fun to surprise others with fun gifts, and it's good for you too. It takes your eyes off of yourself. It also shows you that people around you have needs and wants too.

Who can you bless today? Don't please yourself. Please them instead.

Sometimes my reasons for asking for stuff are wrong, Lord. I'll admit it. Help me to focus on pleasing others. Amen.

DAY 173

A FRUITY GIRL

But the fruit that comes from having the Holy Spirit in our lives is: love, joy, peace, not giving up, being kind, being good, having faith, being gentle, and being the boss over our own desires. The Law is not against these things.

GALATIANS 5:22–23

Imagine you planted a peach tree. You couldn't wait for those peaches to appear. One year went by. A second year went by. Still no peaches.

You would get pretty depressed looking at a tree that refused to do its job! (*You had one job, tree! You were supposed to give me peaches!*)

In some ways you're like that peach tree. God wants you to produce fruit in your life—love, joy, peace, kindness, and so on. If you do your job, the Lord is very pleased. But if you don't produce these fruits, you're kind of like that stubborn peach tree.

Be a fruitful girl. God made you to be fruity. It takes courage, but with the help of the Holy Spirit, you can do it!

I get it, Lord. I need to produce fruit like a healthy tree! May Your Holy Spirit develop abundant fruit within me. Amen.

DAY 174

FEAR, BE GONE!

For God did not give us a spirit of fear. He gave us a spirit of power and of love and of a good mind.
2 TIMOTHY 1:7

Sometimes you get scared. Everyone does, even grown-ups. When it happens, your knees knock. Your hands tremble. You feel like you can't breathe. Your courage has disappeared!

It's easy to get scared when you hear a noise in the night or if something bad happens. But when you start to be fearful all the time, that's not good.

God didn't give you a spirit of fear. That means He doesn't want for you to go around panicking all the time about every little thing. He wants you to put your trust in Him. He's your protector. Whatever you're facing, no matter how frightening, it's not bigger than God.

The Lord gave you a spirit of power and love and a good mind. That means you're bigger than the boogie man. Seriously! The Spirit of God lives inside of you and you're a powerful girl! So, let that fear go. . .in Jesus' name!

Today I let go of my fear. I trust You, Lord. Amen.

DAY 175

EVERYTHING FROM NOTHING

In the beginning God made from nothing the heavens and the earth.
GENESIS 1:1

Before the world was created, there was nothing but darkness. God existed. . .and the angels too. But there was no sky, no earth, no people, no animals, no rivers, no mountains. . .nothing but darkness.

Then God spoke and made everything out of nothing.

Wow. . .think about that! If you were going to bake a cake you would use something (eggs, flour, butter, and sugar). You couldn't just whip up a cake out of thin air could you? What God did sounds impossible, but here's the cool part—we serve a miracle-working God. The same God who made everything out of nothing made you. And He breathed life and courage into you. Isn't it amazing to think that He cared enough about you to think the world needed you?

Thank You God for making everything. I love looking at the rivers and the oceans and all of nature. I'm glad you thought of making me too. I love it here, Lord. Amen.

DAY 176

EVERY PART

Be holy in every part of your life.
Be like the Holy One Who chose you.
1 Peter 1:15

God expects all of His kids to be holy of course. (To be holy means you are pure—you are like Jesus.) But why do you think God added the words "in every part of your life"?

Maybe it's because there are some parts of your life where it's pretty easy to be holy and others where it's really hard.

Example: It's easy to live a Christian life when you're at church or at home. But it gets a lot harder when no adults are around. When they're with you, you try so hard to do the right things. But when they aren't there, sometimes you slip up.

Being holy "in every part" means even in your thoughts, not just your actions. If your thoughts are holy, then you won't be tempted to do the wrong thing when your parents are looking the other way.

What about you? Are you holy. . .in *every* part?

I want to be holy no matter what—when my parents are there and even when they're not. Help me, I pray. Amen.

DAY 177

CALLED TO DO BIG THINGS

Jesus said to them, "Follow Me. I will make you fish for men!" At once they left their nets and followed Him.
MATTHEW 4:19–20

Jesus was walking by the Sea of Galilee when he saw two men (brothers) named Simon and Andrew. They were just dropping their nets into the sea when Jesus came along. As far as we know, they had never even met Jesus before.

Jesus walked up to them and said something that must have sounded very strange: "Follow Me. I will make you fish for men!"

Fish for men? Sounds kind of confusing, doesn't it? Jesus was saying, "Give up what you're doing and come help Me share the good news that I'm the Savior."

When the men realized this, they dropped their nets and said, "You bet! We will follow You." And that's exactly what they did. They became two of His disciples.

Has Jesus ever asked you to do something big and exciting? If so, did you do it?

Lord, You want me to do big things for You. I'm ready to drop my net and follow You! Amen.

DAY 178

GOD WON'T QUIT

I am sure that God Who began the good work in you will keep on working in you until the day Jesus Christ comes again.
PHILIPPIANS 1:6

Have you ever started a job but not finished it? Maybe you started to help your dad clean out the garage but you got distracted and played video games instead. Or maybe you started putting together a puzzle but you got bored and quit.

Finishing what you start is important when it comes to the big things—obeying your parents, doing school assignments, and so on.

Did you know that God always finishes what He starts? It's true. When He makes up His mind about something, He does it all the way. He won't quit. He won't give up.

Learn from Him. Follow His example. God wants you to be a good finisher, not just a good starter.

Lord, I get it! You started a good work in me and You're going to finish it. You want me to do the same thing. I'll do it, Lord! Amen.

DAY 179

ADOPTED!

See what great love the Father has for us that He would call us His children. And that is what we are. For this reason the people of the world do not know who we are because they did not know Him.

1 John 3:1

Imagine your family decides to foster a baby boy. He comes to stay at your house for a few months and starts to feel like part of the family.

Now imagine that your parents get the chance to adopt that baby. They decide to do it and you're so excited! He's really, truly going to be your brother.

Your family goes to court and the judge makes the adoption final. You can hardly believe it the first time you hear your mom say, "That's my boy!" He's her child, part of the family.

That's what it's like when God adopts you into His family. You become His child. He says, "That's My girl!" with the same love in His voice that your mother uses for her new baby boy.

Isn't it great to be loved by your Daddy-God?

I'm Your child and I'm so glad You adopted me, Lord! Amen.

DAY 180

WATCH CLOSELY

Keep awake! Watch at all times. The devil is working against you. He is walking around like a hungry lion with his mouth open. He is looking for someone to eat.

1 Peter 5:8

Have you ever wondered what the devil looks like? We can't see him with our own eyes, but he's hard at work, trying to get people to do the wrong things—to lie, cheat, and steal. He's a major enemy and you need to watch out for him.

This verse says that the devil is kind of like a roaring lion. He walks around with his mouth open looking for someone to eat. Whoa! Does that mean he's really a lion, about to devour you? Nope. It means he's looking for people to hurt. He wants to make Christians stumble, to do the wrong thing. Why? Because God's reputation gets damaged when Christians mess up.

The devil wants to trip you up—you can count on it. But don't let him! Be on your guard. Shut that lion's mouth once and for all.

I don't want to let the devil trick me, Lord.
I'm keeping watch so he doesn't trip me up. Amen.

DAY 181

LOVING THE TOUGH ONES

If a person says, "I love God," but hates his brother, he is a liar. If a person does not love his brother whom he has seen, how can he love God Whom he has not seen?
1 John 4:20

Here's a question: You say you love God, but do you really? Sure, you spend time praying. And yes, you tell people about Him. But if you really, truly love God, that means you love the people around you too.

It's not always easy, is it? Some people make it hard. . .*really* hard. Maybe you look at the bullies at your school and say, "I could never love someone like that."

Believe it or not, God loves all kinds of people—even bullies. In fact, His great love may win them over in the end.

Will you help God win them over? Will you love, even when it's really, really hard? If you'll do that, you will prove to the Lord that You love Him very, very much.

Lord, I'm going to do my best to love others, even the tough cases! Please help me. Amen.

DAY 182

STAND IN THE GAP

*"You have heard that it has been said, 'You must love your neighbor and hate those who hate you.' But I tell you, love those who hate you. (*Respect and give thanks for those who say bad things to you. Do good to those who hate you.) Pray for those who do bad things to you and who make it hard for you."*

MATTHEW 5:43–44

It's easy to love people who are kind to you, but Jesus wants you to love those who hate you. Ouch!

So how do you love the haters? You can start by not doing paybacks. If they hurt you, don't hurt them back. If they're mean, respond in love.

Next, don't talk ugly about them behind their backs. This is going to be tough, but remember. . .God loves those people very much.

Most of all, pray for them. They need your prayers. Someone needs to stand in the gap for them so that they can come to know Jesus. Will you be that someone?

Lord, I'll be that someone. I'll be the one who prays for my enemies and loves those who've hurt me. Amen.

DAY 183

ALL MEANS ALL

For all men have sinned and have missed the shining-greatness of God. Anyone can be made right with God by the free gift of His loving-favor. It is Jesus Christ Who bought them with His blood and made them free from their sins.
ROMANS 3:23–24

Admit it: You mess up at times. You feel pretty awful when you've made a mistake. You didn't mean to mess up, after all. Now you wish you could have a do-over.

God wants you to know that everyone messes up. This verse says that *all* men (and women and children) have sinned. All means *all*. You're not alone.

Whew! It's good to know you're not the only one who makes mistakes, right? But here's the really good news: When you do get it wrong, you get a second chance. Jesus died on the cross to forgive your sins. When you put your trust in Him, all of your mess-ups get washed away. He forgives you and you get to start over.

Whew! I'm so glad You forgive me, God. I've messed up a lot. But I put my trust in Your Son. Amen.

DAY 184

WHAT IS COURAGE?

"Have I not told you? Be strong and have strength of heart!"
JOSHUA 1:9

Have you ever stopped to think what it means to be courageous? Webster's Dictionary defines *courage* as the "mental or moral strength to persevere and withstand danger, fear, or difficulty." That simply means when things get dangerous or scary, you're brave enough to face your fears.

Is it easy to be courageous? No way! But being courageous shows that you're strong.

Have you ever exercised your muscles to make them stronger? Maybe you've practiced a complicated move for dance or gymnastics until you could perform it flawlessly. Or if you're on the soccer field or basketball court, you keep practicing until you're strong enough to keep running in a game.

In the same way, to be strong and courageous, you'll need some practice. The more you step out and bravely try new things, the more courageous you'll become. You'll get stronger and braver every time!

Father, I pray You'll help me trust You to become more courageous. Please help me be braver! Amen.

DAY 185

A SAFE PLACE

As for God, His way is perfect. The Word of the Lord has stood the test. He is a covering for all who go to Him for a safe place.
PSALM 18:30

You might have noticed that following Jesus isn't the most popular thing in the world. In fact, it never has been. If you read the New Testament, you'll find plenty of believers who got in big trouble for following Christ. Some were arrested and put in prison, while others were even killed. That kind of trouble has happened to Christ followers throughout history.

You may not be arrested for your love for Jesus today, but people who don't love Him might make fun of you, treat you differently, or try to do bad things to you.

Even when it's not popular to follow Jesus, keep following Him! Jesus loves when you keep following and loving Him no matter what. If and when you get in trouble for believing in Him, remember that God is a safe place. He's perfect, His Word is true, and He will protect your soul even when people try to hurt you.

Father, thank You for Jesus. Please help me bravely follow Him no matter what. I'm glad You are my safe place. Amen.

DAY 186

WHY WORRY?

"Do not worry about tomorrow. Tomorrow will have its own worries. The troubles we have in a day are enough for one day."
MATTHEW 6:34

It can be so easy to worry! But when you're worrying, you're busy focusing on what *might* or *could* happen. None of the worries have actually happened, though.

While it's usually a good thing to have an active imagination, you need to be careful how you use your imagination. If you're imagining a story for creative writing or what you'd like to be when you grow up or how you can make the world a better place, that's all good. But if your imagination is filled with scary thoughts about things that *could* happen, it's time to stop that daydreaming and remember what's true.

You don't have to worry about tomorrow. In fact, Jesus said *not* to worry about it. It takes a lot of courage to focus on what's true about today. But when you're brave and trust that God will take care of your tomorrow, you won't need to worry.

Father, thank You that You free me from worry. I trust that You have everything under control. Amen.

DAY 187

BAD NEWS

When I am afraid, I will trust in You.
PSALM 56:3

It's never easy to get bad news. Even if you expect and prepare to hear something bad, it's still tough. And usually the bad news leaves you feeling scared or sad.

Whether you hear about something that happened on the news or get a surprising phone call or find out something you didn't want to at the doctor's office, you'll need a little time to think about what has happened. You'll need to give yourself time to be sad or mad. And you'll need to let go of feeling like you are in control and trust God instead.

The good news is that even when you're afraid (*especially* when you're afraid), you can remember who is in control. Your heavenly Father is! Tell Him exactly how you're feeling. Tell Him you're scared. Then decide to trust Him in this scary time, no matter what may happen.

Father, I hate hearing bad news.
When I feel afraid, help me to trust in You. Amen.

DAY 188

ALL YOU NEED TO DO IS ASK

God is our safe place and our strength.
He is always our help when we are in trouble.
Psalm 46:1

A lot of times, being courageous happens when you're facing a crummy situation. You might feel really, really sad, or mad, or nervous, or downright scared. Maybe someone has let you down, or you're asked to do something that terrifies you, or you've received some majorly bad news. After all, you usually don't need to be brave for something you're looking forward to doing. Have you ever needed to be courageous about celebrating your birthday? Or looking forward to Christmas morning?

When you need to be courageous, you need to know you don't have to be brave on your own. God wants to help you all the time, but especially when you're in trouble. When you're facing something you never wanted to face, God is your strength. When it feels like everything in your life is topsy-turvy, God is your safe place. You don't have to face difficulties on your own. He's always there, ready to help you. You just have to ask Him for His help!

Father, I need You to be my safe place, my strength, and my help. Amen.

DAY 189

BEAUTIFUL FEET

How beautiful on the mountains are the feet of him who brings good news, who tells of peace and brings good news of happiness, who tells of saving power.
Isaiah 52:7

Take a look at your feet. Have you ever thought they're beautiful?

Isaiah says that feet are beautiful when they bring good news of happiness, peace, and saving power. That good news is all about Jesus! He's the one who brings happiness and peace. He's the one who saves. Every time you tell someone else about Jesus, your feet turn beautiful.

The thing is, sometimes you might feel a little nervous to tell others about Him. But so many amazing things will happen when you're courageous enough to tell someone else about Jesus.

As you bravely tell about His saving power and peace, remember you're bringing good news. Good news is meant to be shared. . .because it's good! When you do share it, you can wiggle your toes and remember that your feet are starting to look very beautiful!

Father, thank You for the good news of Jesus! Please help me to share it with others. Amen.

DAY 190

ALWAYS LISTENING

I called to the Lord in my trouble. I cried to God for help. He heard my voice from His holy house. My cry for help came into His ears.
Psalm 18:6

Picture this: You're in the middle of taking a test, and your mind goes blank. You have absolutely no idea what to answer and you wish you could vanish from the entire situation.

What do you do? You could put your head down and cry or you could run out of the room, but both of those choices would make a big scene and never really solve the problem of taking the test.

Or you could dig deep to find enough courage to stay there and take the test. As you decide to stay and endure (that just means you stick with it or live through it), pray for help! Ask God to give you the courage to stay and to help you figure out the right answers. Then try your best. Call to Him in your trouble and ask Him for help. He'll listen every single time.

Father, thank You for hearing every single one of my prayers! Amen.

DAY 191

ARE YOU TOO YOUNG?

Let no one show little respect for you because you are young. Show other Christians how to live by your life. They should be able to follow you in the way you talk and in what you do. Show them how to live in faith and in love and in holy living.
1 TIMOTHY 4:12

Do you ever feel like older people don't take you seriously because you're young? Maybe you don't feel like your opinion matters. Or maybe you're tired of being told you're too young.

But you have thoughts and opinions. You know what you like—and don't like. And you might even know that you love Jesus with all of your heart. You want to do what He says too, even if it's hard.

Even if people think or say you're too young, bravely stand for what you believe in. Don't be afraid to say or do the right thing. As you choose to courageously live out your faith in Christ in your words and actions, you'll become an example for other people, no matter what your age.

Father, I thank You that my age doesn't matter to You. You know I love You and want to follow You. Please help me to do that—and to be an example to everyone. Amen.

DAY 192

BRAVER THAN YOU KNOW

For God did not give us a spirit of fear. He gave us a spirit of power and of love and of a good mind.
2 Timothy 1:7

What's the bravest thing you've ever done? Think back on all of your life—what were you most scared to do? Did you need to do something mega-brave, like face a really uncomfortable surgery? Were you super courageous and got up in front of a crowd to give a report or performance? Did you bravely ride a super scary roller coaster?

If you know and love Jesus, you can know that God doesn't give you a spirit of fear. Instead, He fills you with bravery! He'll give you a spirit of power, love, and a good mind too. Through His power (and not your own), you can bravely face any scary thing that comes your way!

Father, thank You for not giving me a spirit of fear! Please help me to remember You've given me a spirit of power, love, and a good mind. Amen.

DAY 193

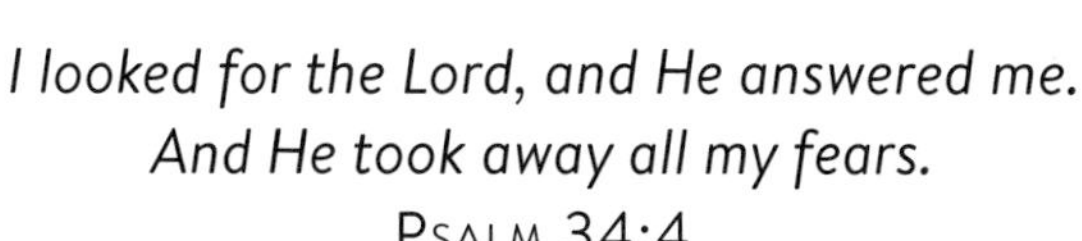

I looked for the Lord, and He answered me.
And He took away all my fears.
Psalm 34:4

Think about a time when your teacher or coach asked you to work on an assignment that seemed pretty impossible. Was it tempting to give up before you even got started? Did you spend more time complaining than jumping right into the challenge?

It's natural to try to resist challenges and wish things were easy. But working through tough times brings a ton of rewards. With a lot of time, practice, and hard work, you can do a lot more than you expect.

The next time you feel overwhelmed by what your coach is trying to teach you, pray for courage and help in figuring things out. When a teacher piles on long, tricky assignments you feel like you can never finish, pray for courage to work hard instead of complaining. Then get busy! You might surprise yourself with what you can do when you work hard.

Father, I'm glad You can take away my fears. Please help me to bravely work hard for You. Amen.

DAY 194

CHOOSE YOUR OWN ADVENTURE

Trust in Him at all times, O people. Pour out your heart before Him. God is a safe place for us.
PSALM 62:8

Have you ever wished you knew just what to do? Or have you wished life was mapped out a little like a board game, and all you need to do is follow along?

You've probably figured out life isn't like that. You'll need to make choices every single day—choices in what you say, do, and think.

Fearing you might not make the right choice can be unsettling. You'll especially need a lot of courage when you just don't know what to do but need to make a decision anyway. In those times when you're feeling confused or wish you knew what to do, pour out your heart to God. He's your safe place.

As you're pouring out your heart to Him, trust Him too. He'll help guide you along all of the twists and turns in your life.

Father, thank You for giving me the freedom of choice. Sometimes I wish I knew what to decide! Please help me make wise choices and remember to trust You all the time. Amen.

DAY 195

CHOOSE YOUR WORDS

He does not hurt others with his tongue, or do wrong to his neighbor, or bring shame to his friend.
Psalm 15:3

How many times have you said something you didn't really mean to say? Words have a funny way of flying out of your mouth. And if you're not careful in choosing what you say, your quickly spoken words can hurt other people.

The old saying "Sticks and stones may break my bones, but words will never hurt me" isn't true. Words *can* hurt. If you're trying to live in a way that shows you love Jesus, you need to love other people too. And that love begins with your words.

Try to help people with the words you say instead of hurting them. When you're tempted to say something mean or cruel, stop yourself. Be brave enough to think about the words you'd like to say—and then choose your words carefully. When you're courageous enough to build people up with your words instead of tearing them down, you'll start noticing the best in people. And they'll notice the best in you too.

Father, please help me to choose words that truly help other people and make You happy. Amen.

DAY 196

DESPERATE

But I am poor and in need. Hurry to me, O God!
You are my help and the One Who takes me out of trouble.
Psalm 70:5

If you've ever known what it's like to not have money (like you have no idea how your parents will be able to buy food for your next meal), you know how desperate that feels.

When you're poor, you know you're in need. And it's scary to wonder how in the world you'll live. How will your mom or dad pay the bills? Where will you live? What will you eat?

Knowing you're out of money is terrifying. You need a lot of courage to keep going. You need to be brave enough to look for help and accept help from other people. And you need endurance to keep going even if you need to sleep or eat in places that might seem scary.

If you know you have nothing, remember you're not completely alone. You have God—and He will be your help. He will be the one who takes you out of trouble.

But if you don't have to worry about money right now, thank God and look for ways to help others who have less than you.

Father, You know what I need. Please help me bravely wait for You to provide. Amen.

DAY 197

DON'T STOP

Never stop praying.
1 THESSALONIANS 5:17

When you're scared, you need to decide what to do. How should you react? How can you face your fear? Sometimes you need to respond right away. But other times, you can take a moment to think about what to do.

When you don't need to make an instant decision, the best thing to do is pray. Praying is simply talking to God. You don't have to get on your knees, fold your hands, or even shut your eyes. You can pray to God out loud, or you can think a prayer.

God knows what you're going through, and He loves you and wants to help you. When you pray, you're simply talking to Him. You can ask for help or tell Him you're scared or thank Him when something's right.

Your prayer doesn't need to be fancy—just talk to Him! And do it as often as you can. As you pray more and more, not only will you start noticing the way He answers your prayers, but you'll also feel a lot of peace about what happens in your life.

Father, I'm glad I can pray to You at any time. Thank You for listening to me! Amen.

DAY 198

HELP!

Show Your great loving-kindness. You save by Your right hand the people that come to You for help from those who hate them.
PSALM 17:7

Sometimes in life, you'll meet people who want the worst for you. No matter what you do, they go out of their way to make your life more difficult. They might come right out and bully you, or they might consider themselves your rival and sneakily try to make sure they're getting the best—not you.

When you come across people who just don't like you, it's tempting to dwell on their bad feelings. You might even wonder how you could change so they'll like you more.

There's no guarantee that everyone will like you and appreciate you in this life. The guarantee, though, is that God will save you from those people who would like to see you stumble and fall.

When you have the courage to keep loving God and following Him with the words you say and the things you do, He'll help you. Your worth is found in Him, anyway—not in what other people say or think about you.

Father, I'm so glad You love me. Please protect me from people who don't like me. Amen.

DAY 199

THE COURAGE TO BE A GOOD FRIEND

A friend loves at all times. A brother is born to share troubles.
PROVERBS 17:17

Friends are amazing gifts from God. If you have a good friend who is kind, dependable, and trustworthy, be thankful, because friends like that are hard to find.

Just as it can be hard to *find* a good friend, it also can be hard to *be* a good friend. When you're grumpy or feeling pressured by others, sometimes you may not be as kind or dependable as you'd like. You might even hurt your friend's feelings.

It takes a lot of courage to choose to do what is right. And it takes a lot of courage to choose to be a good friend.

For the friends you do have, be brave enough to be a true friend. Be worthy of their trust. Speak kind words *to* them—and speak kind words *about* them. Choose to be someone your friends can depend on. Share their troubles by being a good listener. Pray for your friends—and ask the Lord to help you be a good friend.

Father, please bring good, true friends into my life. Please help me to be a good friend too! Amen.

DAY 200

FEAR FACTOR

The Lord is my rock, and my safe place, and the One Who takes me out of trouble. My God is my rock, in Whom I am safe. He is my safe-covering, my saving strength, and my strong tower.

Psalm 18:2

Life can be scary, can't it? Maybe you have a fear of spiders or snakes or the dark. Or maybe you worry about what might happen in the future, what's going on in the world, or what's happening to a family member.

You could spend all day thinking about those fears—and feel even more worried and fearful. Or you could give those worries to the Lord. That simply means you pray and tell God what you're afraid of, then ask Him to take care of those worries for you. If you get tempted to think about those fears again, ask for God's help again until your fear disappears.

God is your safe place. He will take you out of trouble. He's your saving strength. His safety and rescue and strength will make your worries vanish.

Father, I'm glad You are so strong! And I'm glad I can depend on You. Thank You for taking me out of trouble and keeping me safe. Amen.

DAY 201

HARD WORK

Whatever work you do, do it with all your heart.
Do it for the Lord and not for men.
Colossians 3:23

What is your toughest subject in school? Because it's difficult for you, do you usually get excited to do your homework in that subject? Can you hardly wait for that certain class to begin each school day?

It's totally normal *not* to get excited about things that are difficult. In fact, it's pretty uncommon to want to do something that's a challenge. Sometimes you might even want to give up. After all, if something is confusing or difficult, why even try? Why work hard?

It takes a lot of courage to keep trying. You'll need to be brave to work hard and figure out your schoolwork. But all of that courage is good! God is happy when you work hard. In fact, whether your work comes easy to you or is a challenge, you're supposed to do it with all of your heart, imagining that you're working for your heavenly Father and not for your teacher, your parents, or anyone else.

Father, thank You that I can work.
Please help me work hard and remember that
I'm working for You—not for others. Amen.

DAY 202

THE COURAGE TO FORGIVE

O my God, take me from the hand of the sinful, from the hand of the wrong-doer and the man without pity. For You are my hope, O Lord God. You are my trust since I was young.

PSALM 71:4–5

Believe it or not, everyone has had to deal with a bully. Maybe someone has said something horrible to your face. Maybe they've made fun of you behind your back. Or they might even try to physically hurt you. Bullies are mean. And it's hard to figure out what to do when you're being bullied.

But do you know what's even harder? Finding the courage to forgive people who bully you.

Forgiveness is never easy, because it means that in some way, you've been wronged. After all, you never have to forgive people who have made your life better. As you deal with bullies, though, remember that the Lord is your hope and trust. He will protect you. And He will help you bravely begin to forgive others for the wrong things they say or do.

Father, thank You for forgiving me when I've said and done things that have hurt You. Please help me forgive others. Amen.

DAY 203

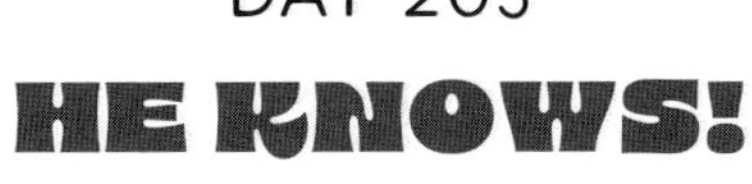

HE KNOWS!

All the days of my life were written in Your book before any of them came to be.
PSALM 139:16

Have you ever had one of those days when you wish someone else knew what you were going through? Maybe everything seemed to go wrong. Or you felt frustrated or lonely or sad and you wished someone could understand exactly what you faced.

Guess what? Your heavenly Father knows! In fact, Psalm 139 tells all about how well He knows you. (If you read the whole psalm, you'll be blown away by how much He knows about you!)

On your crummiest days—and on your best ones too—remember that God knows what is happening. He knows how you'll react and even what you'll say. He knew the day you would be born, and He knows the day you'll die. None of it is a surprise to Him.

The fact that God knows you so well can give you confidence and courage when you need to face all the moments in your day.

Father, I'm glad You know me so well. Please help me trust in You and Your plan for my life. Amen.

DAY 204

HONEST ANSWERS

"He that is not honest with little things is not honest with big things."
Luke 16:10

Honesty is always right. But honesty is not always easy.

Sometimes when you're talking with your parents, they may ask you questions you'd rather not answer. You might even be tempted to answer dishonestly. (Especially if you know you'll get in trouble by telling what really happened!)

But telling the truth is right. And as you talk with your parents, don't be afraid to share what's really on your mind. Courageously tell them the whole story—what you're really thinking, what other people are saying or doing, and what you're tempted to say and do.

As you bravely talk honestly about what's on your heart, you'll discover that when you're honest in these little things, you'll gain trust with your parents. They'll end up trusting you more because they'll know you'll be honest in big things too.

Father, it's not always easy to be honest, but I know it's important to You. Please help me find the courage to answer others honestly. And especially help me be honest with my parents. Amen.

DAY 205

FRIENDS FOREVER?

Happy is the man who does not walk in the way sinful men tell him to, or stand in the path of sinners, or sit with those who laugh at the truth. But he finds joy in the Law of the Lord and thinks about His Law day and night.

Psalm 1:1–2

Picking the right friends can be really hard, especially if you want friends but can't seem to find any who understand you. It's easy to get pulled into groups that aren't exactly the right fit. You want to get along with them, and you want friends, but some girls are mean. They might treat other girls differently than you know you should. Or they might say or do hurtful things, even to you.

If you find yourself stuck with friends who you know aren't the right ones to have, you will need a lot of courage to break off those bad friendships and find some good friends. You might end up feeling lonely. Or your old, not-so-great friends might say bad things about you. Even when it hurts, the Bible promises you'll be happy when you choose to stop hanging out with the wrong crowd.

Father, please bring good friends into my life and help me be a good friend to other girls. Amen.

DAY 206

COMPLETE TRUST

"Do not be afraid, Abram. I am your shield, your very great reward."
GENESIS 15:1 NIV

If you've ever read Genesis, you probably noticed how God set Abram apart. God made huge promises (and He kept them!), but He asked Abram to trust Him in faith. In the same way, God asks you to trust Him in faith. (Faith is complete trust or confidence in someone or something.)

Trusting God in faith can be hard, though! Situations may seem impossible, and sometimes it may feel like you're waiting forever for something to happen, but God is at work. You don't have to worry about the way things will turn out. Just trust Him!

As you trust Him, remember that He'll protect you. He's your shield! Plus, He is your very great reward, worth more than all the stuff of this world. That reward makes all your trust worth it!

Father, I trust You! Thank You for being my shield and very great reward. Please help me not to be afraid, because I know You will protect me. Amen.

DAY 207

HURTFUL HEARING

O God, hear my voice when I complain. Keep my life safe from the fear of those who hate me. Hide me from the secret plans of the sinful and from the noise of those who do bad things. They have made their tongues sharp like a sword. They use poison words like arrows.

PSALM 64:1–3

Hearing other people say mean, hurtful things about you is awful. Hurtful words can leave you feeling like you've been cut by a sword or shot by arrows.

It takes a whole lot of courage to face people when you know they've said or heard mean things about you. When that happens, though, you can tell God exactly how you're feeling.

The writer of Psalm 64 requests, "Keep my life safe from the fear of those who hate me." It can be easy to fear people who hurt you with their words. But God can keep you and your life safe from that fear. He knows what is true about you. He can protect you. And He can heal your heart from the pain of cruel words.

Father, You are truth, and You know what is true. I'm glad You know me, You love me, and You protect me, no matter what anyone else says about me. Amen.

DAY 208

IF I ONLY HAD THE NERVE

"Be strong and have strength of heart. Do not be afraid or shake with fear because of them. For the Lord your God is the One Who goes with you. He will be faithful to you. He will not leave you alone."

DEUTERONOMY 31:6

If you've ever watched *The Wizard of Oz*, the Cowardly Lion is one character who's hard to forget. Even though he did all sorts of brave things, the lion thought he was a coward. In fact, as he quaked with fear, all he wanted was the Wizard of Oz to grant him "the nerve."

Cowardice means you lack bravery. But even if you feel like a coward, you might have a lot more bravery—and nerve—than you realize. Like the Cowardly Lion, you may do really brave things without realizing it. You never have to be afraid, because the Lord your God goes with you. He is faithful and will never leave you alone. He is the one who will grant you "the nerve"!

Father, I'm so glad You'll never leave me alone. Thank You that I can find courage in You! Amen.

DAY 209

IMMOVABLE

I have placed the Lord always in front of me.
Because He is at my right hand, I will not be moved.
Psalm 16:8

Have you ever known other girls who tried to pressure you into doing something you knew was wrong? Can you remember how icky it made you feel inside? You know what's right. But if you want to fit in with girls like this, maybe it's worth doing this one wrong thing. Maybe it's okay to make fun of someone else. Or lie. Or steal. Or cheat.

Forget about the maybes. It's *always* better to choose what's right.

When you know in your heart of hearts what is right and wrong, don't give in to pressure from others. (If you think you can't find the self-control to stand strong for what's right, be prepared to suffer the consequences of choosing what's wrong.)

When you choose to place the Lord always in front of you, He'll direct your paths. You'll understand the right way to go. And when you're pressured into choosing what's wrong, you'll have strength, confidence, and courage to stand firm and not be moved from what's right.

Father, please show me what's right and wrong. Help me to stand firm in my right choices. Amen.

DAY 210

IT'S NOT FAIR

The little troubles we suffer now for a short time are making us ready for the great things God is going to give us forever.
2 Corinthians 4:17

Sometimes life doesn't seem fair. If you're going through something difficult right now—if you're really sick or someone you love has died or you can't believe the tragedy that just happened at your home or school or in your neighborhood—life definitely won't seem fair.

The thing is, troubles are guaranteed. In John 16:33, Jesus promised it: "In the world you will have much trouble. But take hope! I have power over the world!"

You need a whole lot of courage when you're suffering and need to be brave through hard times. The silver lining is that all of the troubles you'll face in life are preparing you for great things God will give you. And those great things won't go away—they'll last forever.

Father, thank You that I only have to go through my troubles for a short time—even if they feel like they'll never end. Thank You for promising to give me great things forever! Amen.

DAY 211

I CAN BE YOUR FRIEND

So we can say for sure, "The Lord is my Helper. I am not afraid of anything man can do to me."
HEBREWS 13:6

Think of a girl who doesn't have many friends. It might be someone at school or church or someone in your neighborhood. Maybe she's new, or maybe she's unpopular.

Now that you've thought of that girl, think about what her life must be like with so few friends. Think about how sad and lonely she must feel.

And now that you can imagine that sad loneliness, think of a way to show her kindness. When will you talk with her? How could you be her friend?

Once you've thought of some ways you could be kind, it's time to act. You'll need some courage when you talk to someone you don't know at all, especially if you're shy. But be bold! Remember, the Lord is your helper. When you are kind to others and include them, you're living a life of love. And that is just what Jesus asked His followers to do!

Father, please help me be a friend to the friendless. Please give me courage to be kind. Amen.

DAY 212

JOY IN THE MORNING

But as for me, I will sing of Your strength. Yes, I will sing with joy of Your loving-kindness in the morning. For You have been a strong and safe place for me in times of trouble.
PSALM 59:16

Whether you're a morning person or a night owl, one thing's for certain: It's easier to be more courageous in the morning. There's something about waking up to a brand-new day and its possibilities. But at nighttime, when it's dark and your mind and body are tired after a full day, it's easier to be fearful.

The solution? If you're up at night fretting over your fear, go to bed. Try to fall asleep and think things over in the morning. You'll have a fresh perspective—even thinking about the Lord's loving-kindness comes easier in the morning!

Father, thank You for bringing me joy in the morning. I praise You for Your loving-kindness and strength! Amen.

DAY 213

IT'S TRUE!

I rise before the morning comes and cry for help. I have put my hope in Your Word.
Psalm 119:147

Courage comes when you face your fears. Trying something new or going out of your way to show kindness to others can be downright scary! When you're courageous, though, you do things that scare you.

So what can you do when you need to face your fear?

If you already know you're scared of something and you'll need a lot of courage, look for Bible verses that will help you. (Not sure where to look? Try the verses in this book!)

As you read God's Word, you'll discover what's true. When you write down your favorite Bible verses, carry them with you, and memorize them, they'll be a huge help in scary times. You'll remember the verses just when you need them most, and they'll help keep your mind focused on truth—not a bunch of worries, lies, or fears.

Thank You for Your Word, Father. I pray that Your truth will help me when I need it most. Amen.

DAY 214

KEEP DOING WHAT'S RIGHT

For You have stood by my right actions. You sit on Your throne, and are right in how You judge.
PSALM 9:4

Making the choice between what's right and what's wrong isn't always easy. In fact, even if you *know* what is right, it can be really hard to choose to *do* what is right.

It can take a lot of courage to do the right thing, especially if it doesn't feel easy. Imagine finding a wallet with a $100 bill left behind in a shopping cart. While it would be easy not to tell anyone and stick the money in your pocket, the harder (but right!) thing to do is to take the wallet and all of the money to the store manager.

Sometimes it seems like you're the only one who knows the decisions you make. But your heavenly Father knows what you choose. And when you choose to do the right thing, He stands by you and your right actions.

Father, I know You are right in how You judge. Thank You for standing by me when I make right choices. Amen.

DAY 215

Of what great worth is Your loving-kindness, O God! The children of men come and are safe in the shadow of Your wings.
PSALM 36:7

Have you ever gone bird-watching? If you've had the chance to watch how mother birds protect their young, you might know they cover their babies with their wings. When baby birds rest beside their mom, the mother bird spreads her wings over her babies like a big, comfy blanket.

Just as a mother bird protects and comforts her young with her wings, God does the same for us. When you're hurting or sad and could use some comfort, you can go to God simply by praying to Him. You'll find safety, comfort, and rest in the shadow of His wings—and that will fill you up with courage.

Father, thank You for keeping me safe! I'm so glad You want to comfort and care for me, especially when I'm sad or scared. Amen.

DAY 216

A NEW START

As for me, I will call on God and the Lord will save me.
PSALM 55:16

Going someplace new—whether it's a new school or a new church—can be really scary! Especially if you don't know anyone else, it takes a ton of courage to walk into a new place and face a bunch of strangers.

The awkwardness of being a stranger in a new place really doesn't ever disappear. Even when you grow up, going to new places and seeing strange faces will still make you a little nervous.

But even with all of the courage you'll need to go to new places, some really wonderful things can happen. You might meet some great people and experience some fantastic things.

When you're trying to build up courage to face new situations, pray for the Lord's help. Pray that He'll keep you safe. Pray that He'll bring new friends into your life. And pray that you'll be able to be a good example of what it means to love Jesus even when you're feeling scared.

Father, I'm really scared to try this new adventure. Please help me! I trust that You will keep me safe. And I ask for You to please make this experience better than I can imagine. Amen.

DAY 217

NOT GETTING YOUR WAY

It is God Who covers me with strength
and makes my way perfect.
Psalm 18:32

Imagine getting to do everything you want. You wake up in the morning—when you want—to the breakfast of your choice. All day long you get to do exactly what you want, when you want. And when you wake up the next day, it happens again. . .and again and again.

Does that sound like your real, actual life? Of course not! Life is filled with doing things you may not want to do. Some things are good for you to do, and other things simply need to be done.

As you're in the middle of doing what's asked of you, sometimes you might need a lot of courage. Going to the doctor might be scary. You might dread taking a big test at school. Or talking with the new kid next door might make you feel a little nervous.

You need courage all the time. Everyone does. Courage is important when you need to do something you'd rather not do. The next time you need courage, remember that God is the one who covers you with strength. He's the one who can give you the courage you need.

Father, please help me be strong and courageous! Amen.

DAY 218

NO FEAR

"See, God saves me. I will trust and not be afraid. For the Lord God is my strength and song And He has become the One Who saves me."

Isaiah 12:2

As you read the Bible more and more, one thing you'll notice is a lot of fear. Even the strongest, bravest heroes in the Bible were afraid.

But guess what? Those men and women became the strongest, bravest heroes because they didn't let their fear win. They trusted the Lord. And when they chose to trust Him instead of being afraid, they discovered that He became their strength. He was the one who saved them and did some pretty amazing things through their lives.

The good news is that the same God who worked in the lives of those brave Bible heroes can work in your life too. He will save you. You can trust in Him and not be afraid. He can become your strength and your song. You just need to trust and rely on Him to do the amazing work through you!

Father, You are amazing, and You work powerfully in the lives of everyday people like me. Please help me to trust You! Amen.

DAY 219

ON YOUR MARK

Let us keep running in the race that God has planned for us. Let us keep looking to Jesus. Our faith comes from Him and He is the One Who makes it perfect.
HEBREWS 12:1–2

God has a unique plan for you and your life. Let that truth sink in for a minute. The God of the universe planned a special life just for you. You have different gifts and abilities from other people, and different experiences too. When you add all that together along with the circumstance you're in, you get a picture of the race He's designed for you—and only you—to run.

When you realize God has planned a unique race just for you, you'll be able to find the courage you need when you know He's asking you to do something.

When God opens up an opportunity for you—or slams the door shut—you can rest bravely in the fact that it's part of His plan for you. Instead of worrying about the details, keep looking to Jesus. He's the one who will help you run your one-of-a-kind, God-given race.

Father, please help me bravely keep running the race You've planned for me. Amen.

DAY 220

PERFECT PEACE

You will keep the man in perfect peace whose mind is kept on You, because he trusts in You.
ISAIAH 26:3

When you hear the word *peace*, what do you think of? Peace and quiet? World peace? Peace on earth? Have you ever stopped to think about what peace really is?

Peace is defined as calm or freedom from disturbances. When you keep your mind on the Lord and trust completely in Him, He'll give you perfect peace. That's perfect calm, even if craziness is happening all around you.

As you try to be a courageous girl, you'll discover that perfect peace is a game changer. When you keep your mind on Jesus, you'll be free from worry. When worry isn't in the picture, bravery is a lot easier.

Father, thank You for keeping me in perfect peace! That's an amazing gift. Please help me keep my mind on You. I want to trust You with my whole heart. Amen.

DAY 221

PRAYING AND WAITING

O Lord, the God Who saves me, I have cried out before You day and night. Let my prayer come to You. Listen to my cry.

Psalm 88:1–2

Sometimes when you pray, you'll notice God answers your prayer almost immediately. But other times, answers don't come so quickly. In fact, you might need to keep praying and praying over months and even years before God answers you.

When you need to keep praying, you'll need courage. It takes a brave resolve to keep on asking God for something when you don't get an answer right away. But as you continue to pray (you can call that persisting in prayer) and wait for an answer, you'll get a lot of practice in waiting on God. Waiting isn't always easy, but the wait can help change your heart and bring you closer to God.

Whatever you do, don't stop praying. Cry out to God day and night. He'll listen, even if He doesn't answer right away.

Father, thank You for listening to my prayers. It isn't easy to wait for Your answers. Please help me to wait and remember that You hear me. Amen.

DAY 222

READY OR NOT

Be strong. Be strong in heart, all you who hope in the Lord.
PSALM 31:24

When it comes to courage, here's a secret you might not know: Sometimes you'll feel like you don't want to be courageous or brave or strong. In fact, until you get a lot of practice making brave choices, bravery can seem pretty overwhelming.

Even if you don't feel like you want to be brave, try to be courageous anyway. Be strong—and be strong in heart. Remember that God is the one who makes you strong, so trust in Him. Whether you feel like you're ready or not, make a brave choice and see what happens. You might surprise yourself! Plus, being courageous won't feel so scary the next time you need to be brave.

Father, I do hope in You. Please help me to be strong in heart and to make brave choices, even when I don't feel like it. Amen.

DAY 223

SAFE!

I am kept safe by God, Who saves those who are pure in heart.
PSALM 7:10

Serving people is a wonderful way to show Jesus' love to the world around you. But sometimes your opportunities to reach out to others might take you to communities or areas that seem a little dangerous.

As much as you may want to help out, it can be scary! Especially if you're doing new things in new places. Yet helping others shows them the love of Jesus and may draw them close to Him. Working hard to serve will bless people in ways you may never know.

If you're ready to help but your palms are sweaty and your knees shaky, stop and pray. Pray for courage. Pray for God to keep you safe. Pray for God to bring others to Jesus through your work. Then jump right in and start helping. You might be surprised by what you experience!

Father, I want to help others and show them the love of Jesus. Please use me. Please help me trust You and overcome my fear. And please keep me safe! Amen.

DAY 224

STAND UP, SPEAK UP

I have a safe place in you, O Lord. Let me never be ashamed.
Psalm 71:1

Did you know that more people are afraid of public speaking than of spiders or snakes. . .or even death? Yep. Fear of public speaking is the biggest phobia in America.

Yet talking in front of an audience doesn't have to be awful. In fact, it doesn't even have to be feared. (Here's a super-helpful tip: Start practicing speaking in public now when you're a girl. Then keep practicing as you get older. By the time you're an adult, you'll find out you have nothing to fear.)

As you build your courage in talking and performing in front of people, remember that you have a safe place in the Lord. Pray that the Lord will give you the right words to say and that He'll fill you with courage and strength. Then stand up and conquer that fear!

Father, I'm glad You're my safe place.
Please help me speak boldly in front of others.
I pray You'll never let me be ashamed. Amen.

DAY 225

SURPRISE!

O taste and see that the Lord is good.
How happy is the man who trusts in Him!
Psalm 34:8

If you've ever found yourself in an unexpected situation, you already know you can't plan everything in life. Surprises happen! If some of those surprises are unwanted (maybe it seems like everything you or your parents have planned will *not* happen), try to pause before you react. Instead of complaining or panicking, stop and pray for the Lord to lead you.

As you courageously trust Him to guide you in your choices, you'll see how He will do amazing things through you—even in life's unexpected situations. You'll see how good He is, and you'll see how happy He'll make you when you trust in Him. He can make even the most unexpected situations wonderful!

Father, You are good. I am so happy I can trust in You! Amen.

DAY 226

SWEET DREAMS

You will not be afraid when you lie down.
When you lie down, your sleep will be sweet.
PROVERBS 3:24

Ever have so many nightmares that you dread going back to sleep?

Sometimes sleep can seem anything but sweet. But the Bible gives a prescription for a good night of sleep. Proverbs 3:21–24 says, "Keep perfect wisdom and careful thinking. And they will be life to your soul and a chain of beauty to your neck. Then you will be safe as you walk on your way, and your foot will not trip. You will not be afraid when you lie down. When you lie down, your sleep will be sweet."

When you think carefully and make wise choices, you don't need to worry. Your life will be better, and your sleep will be better too!

Father, please help me to think before I do or say anything. Please help me bravely make wise choices too. Amen.

DAY 227

TAMING BUTTERFLIES

God is able to do much more than we ask or think through His power working in us.
EPHESIANS 3:20

Have you ever noticed that when you get really scared or nervous you get butterflies in your stomach?

You might dread those butterflies because they feel unsettling and you know that whenever you feel them, you're about to do something scary. But here's a secret for taming those butterflies: The next time you get them, remind yourself that you are being brave and trying something new. Know that you are ready for an exciting adventure.

Your butterflies may not happen very often (that's probably a good thing!), but when you do feel them, take a deep breath. Be brave. Pray for God's help and courage. Then see what He can do through you even with all of your butterflies.

Father, I don't like feeling scared and nervous. I'm really glad I can trust You to do so much more than I can even ask or think. Please give me courage when I'm afraid! Amen.

DAY 228

TELL HIM ALL ABOUT IT

Give all your cares to the Lord and He will give you strength. He will never let those who are right with Him be shaken.
Psalm 55:22

Watching someone you love battle sickness is a really sad, really hard thing. You want your family member or friend to get better. You might even wish you were the one who could be sick instead. But sickness happens. And as much as you'd like to wish the sickness away, you can't.

When you're feeling sad or scared that your loved one is so sick, don't try to bottle up your feelings. Get them out! Write about what you're feeling in a journal. Cry. And tell God everything you're feeling. Tell Him all your fears and sadness. Don't hold anything back. Give all your cares and concerns to Him. When you do, He'll fill you with a peace you can't understand, and He'll give you strength and courage to help the sick people you care about so much.

Father, I give You all my worries. Please help me be loving and brave when others need me. Amen.

DAY 229

SUPERHUMAN STRENGTH

I can do all things because Christ gives me the strength.
PHILIPPIANS 4:13

When you start realizing your courage comes through Christ and not yourself, you might wonder just how much courage you could possibly have. How much strength could Jesus give you? Could you become like Supergirl, with super speed, X-ray vision, and the ability to fly?

While you may not suddenly do what's humanly impossible (sorry—you won't be able to leap over buildings in a single bound), the Bible says you can do whatever you need to do because Jesus empowers you.

As you're living for Him, you don't have to worry about doing things in your own strength, because He'll give you all the strength you need. Now that's a pretty amazing superpower!

Father, it's amazing that Jesus will give me the strength to do all things. Please let me use this strength for You. Amen.

DAY 230

THE WAITING GAME

Wait for the Lord. Be strong.
Let your heart be strong.
Yes, wait for the Lord.
PSALM 27:14

Waiting isn't easy. Whether you're waiting in line at the store or waiting for your turn at the playground or waiting for your birthday, it's not usually something you enjoy. For one thing, you just want to hurry up and get to your desired outcome! (It's hard to sit through a family Christmas dinner when all you really want to do is open up your presents!)

But waiting is a part of life—and always will be.

You'll get a lot of practice waiting. But instead of being annoyed and wishing your waiting away, try to wait with courage. Be brave as you're waiting—especially when you need to wait for something that makes you nervous. (Ever wait for a doctor's appointment?) As you practice waiting bravely, you may discover you have a much stronger heart and a lot more patience than you ever thought.

Father, please help me to wait with courage. I may not like to wait, but please help me to be patient anyway. Amen.

DAY 231

NEW HERE?

In God I have put my trust. I will not be afraid. What can man do to me?
Psalm 56:11

Walking into a room where you don't know anyone else can be super scary. But the next time it happens to you, remember that absolutely everyone is new at some point. You're not alone—other people might not know anyone else either!

Instead of being afraid of all the new faces you see, try wondering who will become your friend in the big group of strangers. Who can you get to know by being friendly and saying "hi"? You might be surprised how much you have in common with someone else in the room—or you might learn something brand new if you're different from everyone else.

As you courageously walk into a new situation, remember how you've put your trust in God. He is worthy of your trust. He'll keep bringing new people into your life—people you still need to meet!

Father, I'm glad I can trust in You even when I'm all alone and afraid to meet new people. Amen.

DAY 232

THINK BIG

Our soul waits for the Lord. He is our help and our safe cover.
Psalm 33:20

Have you ever prayed a big prayer? A prayer in which you've asked God to do something pretty spectacular? A prayer in which you've surrendered your hopes and dreams to Him? A prayer in which you've asked to be used by Him?

When you pray for things that only the Lord could do, you'll need to remember two things. First, you'll need some courage to wait for God to answer those prayers. God isn't a genie in a bottle. He doesn't do magic tricks that you can expect if you just wave a wand and say, "Abracadabra." He's the God of the universe and He has His own will and plan. But He also likes for you to trust Him with big matters. Keep waiting on Him.

The second thing to remember is that you'll probably need even more courage if He answers your big prayers. You may be placed in situations where you need a lot of bravery. Be thankful for those opportunities and the ways God will answer your prayers!

Father, even my biggest prayers aren't too big for You. Please help me wait patiently for You. Amen.

DAY 233

TIME FOR A TEST

My Christian brothers, you should be happy when you have all kinds of tests. You know these prove your faith. It helps you not to give up.

James 1:2–3

Are you ever happy to take tests? Do you get really excited when your teacher announces a pop quiz or final exam? If your doctor prescribes a medical test, can you hardly wait for it to happen?

For the most part, tests aren't something people look forward to—not the tests in school or the tests in life. In fact, sometimes you'll need a lot of courage to face all your test taking.

But the Bible says you should be happy when you face a test. Why? Because a test won't only show what you know or what's going on; it will also prove your faith. When you're facing a tough situation, your faith in God during that trying time will help you not to give up.

Father, I need Your help for the tests I need to take. Please help me to trust You in faith. Amen.

DAY 234

TROUBLE

But the saving of those who are right with God is from the Lord. He is their strength in time of trouble.
Psalm 37:39

You know when something's wrong. Maybe you actually hear an alarm go off or you just know something isn't right.

Knowing that something isn't right can be really scary. Should you panic and scream? Curl up and cry? Run around or stay frozen in fear?

All of those reactions definitely seem natural when there's trouble. Yet there's something else you can do. You can try to stay calm. Staying calm in the middle of trouble isn't easy at all, but it's possible. And in your calmness, you can choose to be brave.

Staying calm in the midst of chaos may seem impossible, but if you rely on God to be your strength, He will give you courage every single time. You can be a lot braver and stronger with Him. On your own, you'll probably give in to fear. But with the Lord, you can be brave.

Father, thank You that You will be my strength in time of trouble. I trust that You will make me brave. Amen.

DAY 235

WEARING OUT

Our human body is wearing out. But our spirits are getting stronger every day. The little troubles we suffer now for a short time are making us ready for the great things God is going to give us forever.
2 CORINTHIANS 4:16–17

Wearing out usually isn't something you look forward to doing. If you're running a race or working really hard for a long time, you'll feel worn out. Your energy is zapped. You might lose your breath, and your muscles feel sore.

All human bodies wear out sometime. This reality is a major bummer. But if you trust Jesus and start living for Him, you'll notice your spirit actually gets stronger. . .even when your body starts to wear out.

Sometimes it feels like your spirit could wear out because of the troubles you face. But know that those pains prepare you for something much better than life on this earth. Your spirit is actually getting ready for forever life with Jesus!

Father, I'm glad that even though my body will wear out eventually, my spirit never will. Thank You for making my spirit stronger every day. Amen.

DAY 236

WHAT A RELIEF

Do not worry. Learn to pray about everything. Give thanks to God as you ask Him for what you need.
PHILIPPIANS 4:6

When you worry, you allow yourself to dwell on your troubles and give in to your fears. Your mind gets stuck thinking only about what could happen—and usually the worst that could happen. You keep thinking about how scared you are or how you don't want to do something.

But the Bible clearly tells us not to worry. Why? When you're busy worrying, you're not fully trusting God. You're forgetting that He's in control of everything—and He can work in huge, amazing ways.

The next time you're feeling afraid or worry starts to creep into your thoughts, pray. Pray about everything! And as you're praying, don't be shy. Ask God for what you need, and thank Him too. By asking Him and thanking Him through your prayers, you'll feel a relief and your worry will disappear.

Father, thank You that I can pray to You anytime and about anything. Thank You that I don't have to worry! Amen.

DAY 237

WHAT HOLDS YOU BACK?

I have put my trust in God. I will not be afraid.
PSALM 56:4

What are some goals you've made? Would you like to try out for a sports team or a role in a play? Dive into the deep end of the swimming pool this summer? Study really hard to ace your test?

One thing you'll need to reach your goal is bravery. And one thing that could keep you from working toward your goal is fear. You might be afraid that someone will laugh at you, or that you'll have to work really hard, or that you might fail. Those fears might become so big that you'll never even try to reach your goal.

You don't have to give in to fear, though. In fact, once you put your trust in God, you don't have to be afraid at all. Put in the hard work and go after your goals. Once you start trusting God and working toward your goal, your fear will melt away, just like an ice pop on a hot summer day.

Father, I'm putting my trust in You.
Thank You that I don't have to be afraid anymore! Amen.

DAY 238

WHY ARE YOU AFRAID?

As they talked, Jesus Himself stood among them. He said, "May you have peace." But they were afraid and full of fear. They thought they saw a spirit. Jesus said to them, "Why are you afraid? Why do you have doubts in your hearts? Look at My hands and My feet. See! It is I, Myself! Touch Me and see for yourself."

LUKE 24:36–39

When Jesus died on a cross and was buried, His disciples never imagined He would rise from the dead and live again. So when they saw Him, they were afraid. In fact, they thought they were seeing His ghost!

Jesus asked His scared disciples why they were afraid—and why they doubted. In their fear, they doubted Jesus really could be alive.

But He was alive. And He still is. You don't have to live in fear or worry. When Jesus rose from the dead, He beat what terrifies most people—death. Because He lives today, you can trust Him with your life and future and live courageously. You can have peace.

Father, I'm so grateful Jesus is alive. Thank You that because of Him, I don't have to live in fear. Amen.

DAY 239

WHO CAN YOU TRUST?

The peace of God is much greater than the human mind can understand. This peace will keep your hearts and minds through Christ Jesus.
PHILIPPIANS 4:7

It's tempting to try to trust yourself. You know your own strengths and weaknesses. You think you know what you can handle.

It's also tempting to rely on someone else. Maybe you trust your parents to always make the right decision or provide what you need.

The one who deserves our trust most of all is God. You can trust your heavenly Father and His plan for your life. You can trust Him with your future. You can trust Him with your eternity. (That's forever!)

You'll need courage to trust Him. But as you trust Him more and more, you'll discover a very cool secret: He'll give you a deep peace that's better than anything you can imagine. And that's way better than anything you'll get from trusting in yourself.

Father, I want to trust You. Please give me the courage to trust my whole life to You. Thank You for giving me peace when I do trust You. Amen.

DAY 240

WHAT'S NEW?

Turn Your ear to me, and be quick to save me.
Be my rock of strength, a strong place to keep me safe.
Psalm 31:2

Many times, trying something new can be scary. Maybe some nervousness can be traced to fear of the unknown or uncertainty about whether you'll like it. But whether it's trying new food or meeting a new person or going to a new school, at some point you need to be brave and try.

Trying new things is great, because it brings fun experiences and adventure to your life. Just imagine how boring life would be if you always stuck to the same old things!

When you're nervous about trying something new, try to forget about what seems a little scary and think about what great things could happen. (Even if what happens is less than thrilling, at least you'll have a story to tell and you'll know you've been brave!) Remember you can turn to God. He can be your rock of strength, even when it feels like you're sinking in all the newness. He is your strong place and He can keep you safe.

Father, thank You for being my rock of strength! Please help me bravely try new things. Amen.

DAY 241

WHOM SHOULD YOU FEAR?

The Lord is my light and the One Who saves me. Whom should I fear? The Lord is the strength of my life. Of whom should I be afraid?
Psalm 27:1

Have you ever noticed someone who seems kind of scary? Maybe it's a quiet neighbor who always keeps to herself, or a new boy at school who seems really, really different.

It's helpful to remember a couple of things when you're feeling scared about other people. First, people are just people. God created each of us. Everyone was born. Everyone will die. Everyone needs food and drink and sleep to survive.

The second thing is that a lot of times, people who seem scary really aren't. It's wise not to talk to strangers. And you should ask your parents for help in figuring out how careful you should be around them. But it's also helpful to remember that a lot of people are much kinder than they might seem. So a sad or scary-looking kid might just be having a really bad day and could use a friendly hello.

Father, please help me remember that I don't have to fear anyone. Please help me shine Your light to everyone. Amen.

DAY 242

WHISTLE A HAPPY TUNE

Sing to the Lord. Honor His name.
Make His saving power known from day to day.
Psalm 96:2

If you've ever watched classic musicals, you might have seen *The King and I*. Some lines from one of the musical's songs, "I Whistle a Happy Tune," express the idea that when you feel afraid, if you hold your head up high and whistle, no one will know that you're not confident and happy.

A lot of truth is packed into those lyrics. No one will suspect you're afraid if you act confident. Even if you have to fake it when you're scared, try looking up, smiling, and even whistling a happy tune. As you're busy pretending to be courageous, you might find a lot of courage.

In the Bible, David knew a lot about whistling (and singing!) a happy tune even when he was afraid. He wrote many songs to describe exactly what he was feeling, and they're included in the book of Psalms. You can read how he felt happy or sad or scared or brave or thankful when you read a psalm. Like David, you can sing to the Lord when you need some courage too!

Father, thank You for listening to my songs when I'm scared or brave, sad or happy. Amen.

DAY 243

ALL THAT MATTERS

I hope very much that I will have no reason to be ashamed. I hope to honor Christ with my body if it be by my life or by my death. I want to honor Him without fear, now and always.
PHILIPPIANS 1:20

Not everyone loves Jesus. In fact, in a lot of places around the world, people who don't love Jesus make a lot of trouble for Christ followers.

But even if believers know they could get in trouble for loving and following Jesus, they still do. As you spend more time with Jesus and get closer to Him through praying, reading your Bible, and living your life the way He asks, you'll love Him more and more.

Your love for Jesus and your belief that He is God are strong. In fact, your love for Him can be so strong that you'll want to honor Him without fear. It won't matter if you could get in trouble for believing in Him and following Him, because He'll become all that truly matters.

Father, thank You for Jesus. I want to honor Him in all that I do—whether other people like it or not. Please help me live for Him without fear. Amen.

DAY 244

YOU'RE NOT ALONE

"Do not be afraid or lose faith. For the Lord your God is with you anywhere you go."
JOSHUA 1:9

Challenges seem a lot easier when you're with someone else. Solo adventures are fun, but whenever you try something new, it can be a lot easier if you're with someone you know.

It's easy to feel afraid when it seems like you're all alone. But the amazing news is that you don't ever have to be alone. God loves you so much and has promised that He is with you anywhere you go. He knows it stinks to be lonely or scared. And He doesn't want that for you. He wants to be with you.

The next time you get scared, pray to Him! Praying just means you talk to God. You can pray out loud or think a prayer. Tell God you're afraid. Thank Him that He's there with you and ask Him to help with whatever you're going through.

Father, thank You for being with me anywhere I go! Please help me not to be afraid as I learn to trust You more. Amen.

DAY 245

TELLING THE REAL TRUTH

Jesus said, "I am the Way and the Truth and the Life. No one can go to the Father except by Me."
JOHN 14:6

The Bible says that Jesus is the only way to get to heaven. What do you think about that? A lot of people believe there are many roads to heaven and it doesn't matter what you believe. They think it doesn't matter what religion you adhere to, as long as you care about what you believe. Some say, "As long as you're a good person, you'll go to heaven."

That's not what the Bible says. God's Word tells us there's only one way to get to heaven, and that's to accept Jesus as your Savior. When you do that, you have a one-way ticket to eternal life with the Lord.

The next time someone tells you there are many ways to get to heaven, work up the courage to speak the truth. Tell them about Jesus Christ and how He came to save them. Then pray for that person to come to know Jesus like you do.

Lord, please give me courage to speak the real truth, that there's only one way! Amen.

DAY 246

CONFESS WHAT YOU'VE DONE

It will not go well for the man who hides his sins, but he who tells his sins and turns from them will be given loving-pity.
PROVERBS 28:13

You messed up. You didn't mean to, but you did. You told a little white lie and before long it grew and grew and grew. Your tiny lie turned into a huge one. You hoped no one would ever find out the truth, but now you've been caught. Your mom knows you've been lying. You wish you could take it all back, but it's too late.

Take a look at today's Bible verse. The Word of God says it won't go well for the person who hides his sins. It's better if you confess. Get it off your chest. Tell someone.

Why is it better to get things out in the open? When you confess your sin, God is faithful to forgive. And things will go better with your parents if you're honest too.

No matter what you've been hiding, you can tell someone today. It's going to take courage to come clean, but you'll feel so much better when you do. No more secrets. Tell someone what you've done.

It's not going to be easy, but I'll confess my sins, Lord. Give me courage, I pray.

DAY 247

SPEAK. . .AND ACT

My children, let us not love with words or in talk only. Let us love by what we do and in truth.
1 John 3:18

It's one thing to tell someone you love them; it's another thing to prove it with your actions. What if you said to your friend, "You're my BFF," but then you never talked to her or spent any time with her? Would she believe your words?

If you care about the people in your life (and you do), then do things that will show them how much you care. Would you believe your mom loved you if she said the words "I love you" but never fed you or gave you a place to live? Words need to be followed by actions.

God wants you to follow through. If you say something, prove it. Don't just say, "I'll study for the test." Actually study for the test. Don't just say, "I'll read my Bible and pray"—actually do it. Don't just say, "I'm so glad you're my little brother," unless you treat him the way you want to be treated.

Lord, I get it. My words need actions. It's not enough just to say something. I have to do it. Amen.

DAY 248

THE THINGS GOD HATES

There are six things which the Lord hates, yes, seven that are hated by Him: A proud look, a lying tongue, and hands that kill those who are without guilt, a heart that makes sinful plans, feet that run fast to sin, a person who tells lies about someone else, and one who starts fights among brothers.

Proverbs 6:16–19

Did you know there are things God hates? Today's verse shows us that the Lord can't stand things like pride or lying or murder. He's also not happy when His kids behave wickedly or tell lies about each other.

Why do you suppose God hates these things? After all, God is usually all about love, not hate. He despises these things because they are the opposite of how the Bible tells us to live. The Word of God instructs us not to be prideful. It teaches us to love our enemies. The Bible tells us that lying is wrong. It hurts others and breaks up friendships.

Take a close look at the list of things God hates and make sure you remove them from your life. Replace them with things like love, joy, peace, and hope.

Lord, please remove things like lying and pride from my life. I want to please You, Father! Amen.

DAY 249

COURAGE TO PRAY

Do not worry. Learn to pray about everything.
Give thanks to God as you ask Him for what you need.
PHILIPPIANS 4:6

Did you know that it takes courage to pray? Sometimes when things go wrong, you just want to get upset. You want to worry and fret. The last thing you feel like doing is praying. You're too upset.

But God's Word says to learn to pray about everything. Why do you suppose it says "learn" to pray? Because we have to do it over and over again before it becomes our normal reaction. Worried about an upcoming test? Pray. Worried because your dad lost his job? Pray.

The other part of this verse is important too. God wants you to give thanks to Him as you ask for what you need. Wow! If you ask with a grateful, joy-filled heart, worries will disappear!

I get it, Lord. I don't need to waste my time worrying. You'll give me courage to ask You for what I need. And when I ask, You will fill my heart with gratitude and joy! Amen.

DAY 250

DON'T GIVE IN!

"Watch and pray so that you will not be tempted. Man's spirit is willing, but the body does not have the power to do it."
MATTHEW 26:41

What do you think of when you hear the word *temptation*? Have you ever been tempted to do something wrong? In some ways, temptation is like a bag of sugary treats. You want them so much but you know you shouldn't eat them all because you'll end up with a belly ache.

God knows you will be faced with temptation and He wants you to be strong enough to handle it. That's where prayer comes in. You can pray and ask God to keep you from being tempted. He knows your weaknesses and knows just how to help you.

What's your biggest temptation? Don't give in to it! Why not pray about it instead and let God handle it for you? Sure, it will take courage to do the right thing, but you're a courageous girl!

Lord, I get tempted to do the wrong things sometimes. I'm glad to hear that You want to help me! I don't want to give in to temptation, so I will pray and ask for Your help. Amen.

DAY 251

DON'T GIVE UP!

Be happy in your hope. Do not give up when trouble comes. Do not let anything stop you from praying.
ROMANS 12:12

Have you ever felt like giving up? Maybe your teacher gave you a big assignment, a paper you needed to write by a certain date. You tried to write it, but nothing came out. A couple of days before it was due you tried, tried, tried. . .but it just wasn't coming. Oh, how you wished you could forget the whole thing!

The Bible says, "Don't give up!" Give that project to the Lord and ask for His help. He will give you hope, even in the last few days before it's due. Keep on praying. Keep on asking. With God's help, you'll get everything done. Those words will flow and that paper will be amazing because you kept going, even when you didn't feel like it.

Don't quit. Keep going. God will help you.

Lord, I won't give up. Sure, I'm tempted at times, but You help me finish what I start and I'm so grateful. Amen.

DAY 252

POWER FROM THE HOLY SPIRIT

"But you will receive power when the Holy Spirit comes into your life. You will tell about Me in the city of Jerusalem and over all the countries of Judea and Samaria and to the ends of the earth."
ACTS 1:8

After Jesus died on the cross, He rose again. You probably know that part of the story. But did you know that He sent His Spirit to live inside of His believers a short while later? It happened on the Day of Pentecost. All of the disciples were gathered together in a room where they had been praying. All of a sudden, a crazy-loud wind filled the place and they began to speak in other languages. Everyone was so surprised. They didn't really know what was happening, but they knew it was powerful!

On that amazing day the Spirit filled them with power and boldness. They began to share the gospel everywhere they went.

When you come to know Jesus and give your life to Him, He fills you with His Spirit and enables you to do great and mighty things for Him. If you ever want to know where courage comes from, it's a gift from the Holy Spirit.

Thank You, Holy Spirit, for filling me up to the tippy top. I'm courageous with Your help. Amen.

DAY 253

CHOSEN. . .BUT NOT PRIDEFUL

God has chosen you. You are holy and loved by Him. Because of this, your new life should be full of loving-pity. You should be kind to others and have no pride. Be gentle and be willing to wait for others.

COLOSSIANS 3:12

Did you know that you are called and chosen by God? It's true! He called you to be His child and you are loved by Him. Don't let this special calling give you a big head, though. Don't get prideful about it. Now that God has called you, He wants you to show love to others. And He wants you to let them know that they are chosen by God too!

How do you show love to other people? Offer grace when they mess up. Forgive when they hurt you. Reach out to them when they are lonely. Treat them the way you want to be treated.

Love others the way Jesus loves them. Show them what it means to be a chosen child of God.

Lord, I'm so glad You chose me and You love me. Help me share Your love with others so they can know they are chosen by You too. Amen.

DAY 254

WISDOM FLOWS OUT

She opens her mouth with wisdom.
The teaching of kindness is on her tongue.
PROVERBS 31:26

Take a look at today's verse. Did you know you can open your mouth and wisdom will come flowing out? Oh, I know what you're thinking. When you open your mouth, silly things come out. Happy things come out. Sometimes angry words come out. But with the help of the Lord, you can speak words of wisdom to others.

Wisdom teaches you how to love others first. It says, "You don't always have to be number one." Wisdom teaches you how to treat others with kindness. In fact, you can share that kindness with everyone you meet. When you do, people will know you're very wise indeed.

Lord, I want to be wise. I don't want to say foolish things or hurt other people. I want wisdom and kindness to flow. Amen.

DAY 255

KEEP STANDING

"Those who have it very hard for doing right are happy, because the holy nation of heaven is theirs."
MATTHEW 5:10

Sometimes you do all the right things but a situation doesn't turn out the way you'd hoped. Maybe you share your faith with someone who just makes fun of you. Or maybe you work, work, work to start an after-school Bible club only to be disappointed in the end when other kids won't join you.

It's frustrating, isn't it? And it hurts even more when wicked people seem to get their way. *Ugh.*

Life is like that at times. People take a stand for what's right but end up getting hurt. It stinks!

So what do you do when things don't turn out right for you? First of all, don't get discouraged. Don't get mad. In this life, things won't always work out the way you hope. But remember, one day you will live in heaven. There, everything will be made right.

I won't give up when things don't go my way, Lord. I'll keep taking a stand for You, no matter what. Amen.

DAY 256

HE'S PREPARING A PLACE FOR YOU

"Do not let your heart be troubled. You have put your trust in God, put your trust in Me also. There are many rooms in My Father's house. If it were not so, I would have told you. I am going away to make a place for you. After I go and make a place for you, I will come back and take you with Me. Then you may be where I am."

John 14:1–3

Have you ever thought about what happened to Jesus after He died and rose again? The Bible says He went back to heaven. But He's not just sitting there on His throne. He's working on a very special project just for you.

What sort of project, you ask? He's preparing a place for you in heaven. You're going to have an amazing home when you get there. Jesus is getting things ready right now.

Did you know that Jesus is coming back to get His children and take them to heaven one day? Make sure you're ready for that special day by asking Him to live in your heart.

Jesus, thank You for preparing my house in heaven! I can hardly wait to see it—and You! Amen.

DAY 257

DON'T WORRY!

Worry in the heart of a man weighs it down,
but a good word makes it glad.
PROVERBS 12:25

Have you ever had a really hard day, one when you just couldn't stop worrying about everything? Maybe you worried about your brother because he was sick. Maybe you worried about a bad grade you made in school. Or maybe you couldn't stop worrying because a friend was mad at you. She wouldn't forgive you for something bad you said about her, even though you apologized.

God doesn't want you to worry. He wants you to learn to trust Him instead. The Bible says that a good word will make your heart glad.

Want to know where you can find lots of good words? In the Bible. Take some time every day to read a few of your favorite verses from the Bible out loud. Your worries will disappear as you read those amazing verses.

Lord, I love Your Word! The Bible is filled with so many wonderful verses. I read them and think about them and my worries disappear.

DAY 258

I COME AGAINST YOU IN THE NAME OF THE LORD!

David said to the Philistine, "You come against me with sword and spear and javelin, but I come against you in the name of the LORD Almighty, the God of the armies of Israel, whom you have defied."
1 SAMUEL 17:45 NIV

There's an amazing story in the book of first Samuel where young David, the shepherd boy, comes face-to-face with a giant named Goliath. Some say that Goliath was more than nine feet tall and everyone was terrified of him!

Even though he was just a boy, David wasn't scared. He knew God was on his side. He took five smooth stones, put one of them in his slingshot, and killed that giant dead.

Here are a few "giants" you might be facing in your life: worry, anger, jealousy, depression, or fear. You can do what David did. Tell those giants that they have to go, in Jesus' name. God is on your side!

Lord, I've been fighting so many giants. I'm ready to take them down with Your help. Amen.

DAY 259

NO COMPLAINING!

Do everything without grumbling or arguing, so that you may become blameless and pure, "children of God without fault in a warped and crooked generation." Then you will shine among them like stars in the sky.

PHILIPPIANS 2:14–15 NIV

Are you a whiner? Do you grumble and complain a lot? If someone made you a bet that you couldn't go all day long without complaining, could you do it?

Take a look at today's verse. Jesus wants you to do everything—and that means everything—without complaining. Does that seem impossible?

It's not easy, especially if you have brothers and sisters who live in your house with you. But when you choose peace instead of arguing, you're setting a good example for them. And you are making God smile. When you do that, you will shine like the stars in the sky.

Lord, I need Your help with this one. I'm not sure I can do it on my own. I get a little grumpy sometimes and like to complain. But I want to stop! Amen.

DAY 260

DON'T BOW DOWN

Shadrach, Meshach and Abednego replied to him, "King Nebuchadnezzar, we do not need to defend ourselves before you in this matter. If we are thrown into the blazing furnace, the God we serve is able to deliver us from it, and he will deliver us from Your Majesty's hand. But even if he does not, we want you to know, Your Majesty, that we will not serve your gods or worship the image of gold you have set up."

DANIEL 3:16–18 NIV

Shadrach, Meshach, and Abednego refused to bow down and worship a false god, even when the king told them they had to.

Because they would not bow down, the king threw them into a fiery furnace. In fact, the furnace was hotter than it had ever been. When they were thrown in, an amazing thing happened! They did not get burned. Jesus showed up and kept them safe.

You will go through hard things too, but (as He did for Shadrach, Meshach, and Abednego) Jesus will always show up for you.

Thank You for always showing up for me, Lord. Amen.

DAY 261

GOOD MEDICINE

A cheerful heart is good medicine,
but a crushed spirit dries up the bones.
PROVERBS 17:22 NIV

Have you ever been really sick? Maybe you had a bad cold and high fever. Or maybe you had a stomach bug. Being sick is so icky! You have to stay in bed and you feel just awful. You wonder if you'll ever feel good again.

When you're really sick, the doctor prescribes medicine for you to take. That medicine helps you get better quicker. If you refuse to take it, you could be sick for a long time, or even get worse.

God has special medicine too. It's called laughter! (It's true—laughter is medicine!) When you're happy, you start to feel better inside and out.

The next time you get the giggles, look up to heaven and say, "Thanks for my meds, Lord! I feel better already!"

I get it, Lord. Laughter makes everything better. When I'm having a bad day, the giggles can turn things around. I'm so joyful when I'm with You. Amen.

DAY 262

PLEASING GOD

And without faith it is impossible to please God, because anyone who comes to him must believe that he exists and that he rewards those who earnestly seek him.
HEBREWS 11:6 NIV

Have you ever tried really, really hard to please your parents or teachers, but ended up messing up? Maybe you promised Mom you would stop arguing with your brother and you really tried, but he got on your nerves and you blew it.

The Bible says pleasing God is a good thing, but it's impossible to please Him without faith. You have to believe He's actually there, that He exists. And you have to remember how much He loves you. Just like your mom, He forgives you when you mess up.

You *will* mess up, by the way. Everyone does. Don't get too upset about it. Just apologize and do your best next time. Your parents (and God) will go on loving you, even on the days when you blow it.

Thank You for forgiving me when I mess up, Lord! Amen.

DAY 263

IT'S BETTER TO HAVE JESUS

"What good will it be for someone to gain the whole world, yet forfeit their soul? Or what can anyone give in exchange for their soul?"
MATTHEW 16:26 NIV

Imagine you won a million dollars. How would you spend the money? Would you buy a mansion? Would it have an amazing swimming pool and a media room with the latest smart TV? Would you buy expensive clothes? Would you buy your parents a fancy new car? Oh, the things you could buy with that much money—lots and lots of stuff!

Take a look at today's verse. The Bible says no matter how many awesome things you have in this life, the most important thing is Jesus. Don't ask for stuff—ask for more of Him. It would be better to have Jesus and nothing at all than to have everything in the world and no relationship with Him.

Which is more important to you—Jesus or your stuff?

Lord, You're more important to me than anything. I don't need stuff, but I definitely need You! Amen.

DAY 264

PLAYING FAVORITES

At that time the disciples came to Jesus and asked, "Who, then, is the greatest in the kingdom of heaven?"
MATTHEW 18:1 NIV

Everyone wants to be teacher's pet. Everyone wants to be the favorite.

Why do you suppose that is? Why is it so important to know that you are number one to your parents, your grandparents, and even your teachers? Maybe it's because you want to feel extra special. Knowing you're number one feels good.

The disciples wanted to feel special too. They wanted Jesus to say, "You're My favorite!" That's why they asked Him, "Who's the greatest?" Maybe they were surprised by His answer. Jesus told them the truth, that He loves all people equally. There is no "greatest" with Him. He wants everyone to know that they're His favorite.

Do you love all people equally, or do you treat some better than others? It's time to love like Jesus loves.

Lord, thank You for loving us all the same. I don't have to be teacher's pet with You because I already know I'm loved. Amen.

DAY 265

HE'S POWERFUL WHEN I'M WEAK

But he said to me, "My grace is sufficient for you, for my power is made perfect in weakness." Therefore I will boast all the more gladly about my weaknesses, so that Christ's power may rest on me.

2 Corinthians 12:9 NIV

Have you ever had a day when you just felt like a real weakling? Maybe you didn't want to get out of bed in the morning. You were too tired. Then at school, nothing went your way. Everything you tried to do failed.

What do you do on those weak days? Do you give up? Do you go home and crawl under the covers?

Jesus doesn't want you to give up. He wants to remind you that He's powerful when you're weak. At the very moment you say, "I can't do this!" He says, "That's okay, I can."

God is the strongest of the strong and He wants to work through you. Trust Him, even when you're feeling like a weakling.

I'm glad I don't have to be strong all the time, Lord. When I'm weak, You are strong. Amen.

DAY 266

EYES WIDE OPEN!

Who can see his own mistakes? Forgive my sins that I do not see.
Psalm 19:12

How many mistakes do you think you make every day? Five? Ten? A hundred?

The truth is, we all make mistakes. And some days are harder than others. It's not always easy to see our own mess-ups, is it? (Ick! Life would be so much easier if we were perfect!) Most of the time we notice when we make mistakes, but sometimes we don't even realize we've messed up. We're not paying attention.

God loves you so much that He forgives the slip-ups you do see and even the ones you *don't* see.

He wants you to pay attention, though. Eyes wide open, girl! You want to live a holy life so that you can be a good example to others of what a Christian is like.

God, thank You so much for forgiving my sins—the ones I see and the ones I don't see. Amen.

DAY 267

DRESS IN HIS ARMOR

Finally, be strong in the Lord and in his mighty power. Put on the full armor of God, so that you can take your stand against the devil's schemes.

EPHESIANS 6:10–11 NIV

Read the sixth chapter of Ephesians and you will see that God has given you several pieces of armor, much like a soldier would wear. He's given you a breastplate of righteousness, a helmet of salvation, the sword of the Spirit, and much, much more.

Why do you suppose God has given you armor to wear? Are you supposed to go to war like a soldier? Will you have to fight a real enemy?

In a way, life is a battle. Every day you have to take a stand for what's right. The enemy is trying to take you down. You can fight him with the weapons God has given you. It takes courage to stand up to evil, but God is on your side.

I will use Your armor to take a stand for what I believe, Lord! Thanks for protecting me. Amen.

DAY 268

HE'S THINKING OF YOU

When I look up and think about Your heavens, the work of Your fingers, the moon and the stars, which You have set in their place, what is man, that You think of him, the son of man that You care for him?
Psalm 8:3–4

God is totally amazing and extraordinarily creative! He thought of everything! He hung the moon and the stars in the sky, and they twinkle at night to remind us that He is there. He created the mountains and the rivers and beautiful rainbows after stormy days.

God took the time to create caterpillars and dragonflies, bunny rabbits and porcupines. And even though He was busy with all of that, He decided the world needed a girl like you.

The Lord must be very busy taking care of His creation, but He never stops thinking about you. He loves and adores you so much. Don't you feel blessed knowing that your creative heavenly Father loves you and all the other people He created more than the rest of creation? You are the apple of His eye.

Lord, thank You for thinking of me! I know how busy You must be, but You still take the time to make me feel special and loved. Amen.

DAY 269

GOD IS ON YOUR SIDE

"Lift up your special stick and put out your hand over the sea, and divide it. Then the people of Israel will go through the sea on dry land."
EXODUS 14:16

A group of people called the Israelites were being held as slaves in the land of Egypt, but God told them to bravely leave Egypt and He would lead them to the Promised Land, the place that would become known as Israel.

Along the way, all sorts of miracles took place. God provided food, water, and everything else they needed.

The army of Egypt followed after them because they were so angry to be losing their slaves. When they got to the Red Sea, the Israelites were frightened. How would they ever make it across to the other side? God told Moses, their leader, to hold up his special stick. When he did, God parted the waters and the Israelites walked through the sea on dry ground. When the Egyptian army came behind them, the waters closed up and all of the Egyptians died.

God sure took care of His people, didn't He? He will take care of you too. Don't worry—the Lord is on your side.

Thank You for being on my side, Lord. Amen.

DAY 270

FIRST MOMENTS

Listen to my cry for help, my King and my God. For I pray to you. In the morning, O Lord, You will hear my voice. In the morning I will lay my prayers before You and will look up.
Psalm 5:2–3

What's the first thing you think of when you wake up in the morning? As you lie in bed, do you yawn and stretch? Do you roll over? Do you moan and groan because you're still sleepy? Do you hit the snooze button on your clock?

God wants you to spend your first moments of the day visiting with Him. Have a chat with Jesus before your feet even hit the floor. Tell Him the things you're excited about. Tell Him what's worrying you. Ask for His help in all things. If you are struggling with anything, let Him know first thing and He will show you how to make things right.

Why do you suppose God wants the first moments of your day? He wants to know that He matters most. Give Him those moments and you'll have a blessed day.

Today I choose to give You my first moments, Lord. I'll think of You first! Amen.

DAY 271

THE SIN PIT

See how the sinful man thinks up sins and plans trouble and lies start growing inside him. He has dug out a deep hole, and has fallen into the hole he has dug.
PSALM 7:14–15

Have you ever had a friend who was just plain naughty? Maybe he was always thinking up bad things to do. Or maybe he was always in trouble with his teacher or parent.

Sinful people do wrong things on purpose. They come up with plans that hurt themselves and other people. God doesn't like this kind of behavior. He wants you to make good plans and to treat others with kindness and love. He doesn't want you to fall into a pit like the naughty kids. He wants you to live a holy life, one that honors Him and blesses you. God wants this for you because He loves you.

It takes courage to live a holy life, but you can do it, girl!

I don't want to fall into a sin pit, Lord! I want to live my life in a way that honors You! Amen.

DAY 272

THE BELLY OF THE FISH

The Lord sent a big fish to swallow Jonah, and he was in the stomach of the fish for three days and three nights.
JONAH 1:17

Do you ever feel like running away? Maybe life is hard and you just don't want to face things anymore. You wish you could pack your bags and move to a new place.

That's what happened to a man named Jonah. God told him to do something really hard, something he didn't want to do. Instead of following God's orders, Jonah ran the opposite direction. He ended up on a ship, and soon a big storm hit. Jonah was tossed overboard, and guess where he landed? In the belly of a big fish!

Can you imagine being swallowed by a fish? What?!

God was gracious to Jonah. The fish spit him out and he got a second chance.

What about you? Are you still tempted to run away from the hard things? You don't want to get caught in the belly of a big fish! It's best to obey God right away.

I will obey You, Lord. I will do what's right. Amen.

DAY 273

HIS POWER IS WORKING!

God is able to do much more than we ask or think through His power working in us.
EPHESIANS 3:20

Do you like to watch movies about superheroes? It's amazing to see them climb up the sides of buildings or fly through the air, isn't it? How cool would it be to have superhuman powers?

If you really want to see something supernatural, hang out with God. He can heal the sick, make the blind see, fix broken relationships, and even raise people from the dead! There's no superhero in any movie who even comes close.

Today's verse says that God is able to do more than we could even ask or think. Read the last part of that verse again. He is working *through* us! That means *we* become superheroes when God's Spirit lives inside of us.

God is able to do more than you could ask or think, and He's doing it through you. He has great things in store for you.

You are working miracles all the time, God. And You want to use me to do amazing things too. Wow! Jesus, You really are my superhero. Amen.

DAY 274

LOVE YOUR ENEMIES

If the one who hates you is hungry,
feed him. If he is thirsty, give him water.
Proverbs 25:21

When you're really mad at someone, you don't want good things to happen to them, do you? Sometimes you wish bad people would suffer. But that's not God's way.

Take a look at today's verse. God says, "If the one who hates you is hungry, feed him. If he is thirsty, give him water." Ouch! You mean I have to show kindness and love to the very people who have hurt me?

The answer is yes! That's God's way. Do unto others as you would have them do unto you. Treat them the way you would want to be treated, even if they don't deserve it. *Especially* if they don't deserve it. God will honor your actions, and He might even make that person a friend.

Lord, I will do my best to care for the people who have hurt me. It will take courage and I will need Your help, but I trust You, Lord. Amen.

DAY 275

A SNAKE IN THE GRASS

Then the woman said to the snake, "We may eat the fruit of the trees of the garden. But from the tree which is in the center of the garden, God has said, 'Do not eat from it or touch it, or you will die.'"

GENESIS 3:2–3

You'll find the creation story in the book of Genesis, the very first book of the Bible. God created Adam and Eve, all of the animals, the heavens and the earth, and everything on the earth.

He placed Adam and Eve in a special garden called Eden. In that garden were all sorts of tropical plants and trees. There was one tree in the middle of the garden that they were not allowed to touch. God told them, "Stay away from that one!"

Satan came to Eve disguised as a snake and told her to eat the fruit from that tree. She made a very bad choice. She gave the fruit to her husband and they both ate it. Oops!

God's heart was broken when He saw that His children had disobeyed. From that time until now, God's heart has been broken by all of us. That's why He sent His Son, Jesus, to die for our sins, so that we could be forgiven.

God, I want to live for You. Amen.

DAY 276

BELIEVE, EVEN WHEN YOU CAN'T SEE

We always thank God that when you heard the Word of God from us, you believed it. You did not receive it as from men, but you received it as the Word of God. That is what it is. It is at work in the lives of you who believe.
1 THESSALONIANS 2:13

You can't see God with your eyes, so how can you prove He's really there?

This is where faith comes in. You can see Him with your heart. You can see the wonderful things He has done for your family and friends.

Believing in God takes faith and courage. Take a look at today's verse. God loves when you take Him at His word, when you believe in Him even though you can't see Him.

He's doing great and mighty things in your life. Maybe you can't see them yet, but someday you will. When you are grown up, you will look back on your life and say, "Wow! The Lord has done amazing things in my life!"

Thank You, God, for working in my life. I choose to believe in You, even when others do not. You are faithful and true. Amen.

DAY 277

TRAPPED!

A sinful man is trapped by his sins,
but a man who is right with God sings for joy.
PROVERBS 29:6

Imagine a raccoon was knocking over your trash can every time you put it out. That rascally little creature would dig around inside the can and make a huge mess that your dad would have to clean up the next morning. So Dad decided to set a trap and catch the raccoon. He put a cage out with the food inside and the raccoon fell for it! He ended up inside the cage, not inside the trash can.

In some ways, sin is like that cage. When you sin, you get caught in a trap. It's impossible to get out without God's help, just like it's impossible for that raccoon to get out of the cage without your father's help.

God doesn't want you to be trapped in sin. He wants you to be set free.

What sins have trapped you lately? Maybe it's time to make a list and ask for God's help to be set free.

Lord, I don't like being trapped in sinful behaviors. I want to be set free from all my sins, but I need Your help. Amen.

DAY 278

ONE BODY, DIFFERENT PEOPLE

There are many people who belong to Christ.
And yet, we are one body which is Christ's.
We are all different but we depend on each other.
ROMANS 12:5

"Red and yellow, black and white, they are precious in His sight." Maybe you've sung these words in the song "Jesus Loves the Little Children."

If you look around you, you can't help but notice that people are all very different. Some are tall, some are short. Some are chubby, some are thin. Some have light skin, some have dark skin. Some eat spicy food, some eat bland food. Some live in the mountains, some live on the seashore.

We all live in this big wide world that God created, and He placed every person in it for a reason. He loves everyone equally and wants all of His children to come to know Him.

All around the globe, Christian believers are worshipping Him even now. They are part of your big family. Wow! What a family it is!

Lord, thank You for my big family. Amen.

DAY 279

PEACE IN THE STORM

A furious squall came up, and the waves broke over the boat, so that it was nearly swamped. Jesus was in the stern, sleeping on a cushion. The disciples woke him and said to him, "Teacher, don't you care if we drown?"

MARK 4:37–38 NIV

Jesus and His disciples were in a boat going across the Sea of Galilee. He was taking a nap when a big storm blew up. His disciples panicked. They didn't know what to do, so they woke Him up and said, "Teacher, don't you care if we drown?"

Of course Jesus cared. He just wanted His disciples to have faith and courage and to trust Him, even in the middle of the storm.

He spoke to the storm, saying, "Peace, be still!" At once, the waves stopped rolling and the wind stopped blowing. The disciples were amazed.

Have you been through any storms in your life? Maybe the wind wasn't really blowing and the waves weren't crashing, but you felt unsettled or uneasy. Maybe someone was sick or your dad lost his job.

Don't worry! Jesus is right there with you during your storms, whispering, "Peace, be still."

Lord, I trust You, even in the middle of the storm. Amen.

DAY 280

WHO ARE YOU TRYING TO PLEASE?

Do you think I am trying to get the favor of men,
or of God? If I were still trying to please men,
I would not be a servant owned by Christ.
GALATIANS 1:10

Are you a people pleaser or a God pleaser? People pleasers are always worried about what their friends might think. A God pleaser is only concerned about what the Lord might think.

Imagine you have to sing a solo in front of your class. You do your best, but when it's over, you can't stop thinking about all the mistakes you made. You're worried the other kids will make fun of you. Instead of fretting over them, just think of how proud God is of you. He's tickled that you were brave enough to stand up there and sing! You're His daughter, and you've made Him very happy.

Next time you're tempted to worry about what your friends think, stop and ask yourself, *Does it really matter?* All that matters is what God thinks.

I want to please Your heart, Lord. I don't want to worry about what other people think of me. Amen.

DAY 281

GUARDIAN ANGELS

For he will command his angels concerning you to guard you in all your ways.
Psalm 91:11 NIV

Wouldn't you love to be an angel for a day? It would be amazing to see what they see and do what they do. After all, angels get to spend time in the presence of God and still see what's going on with humans as well. They really get around!

Look around you. Do you see any angels? Can you feel the flutter of their wings? The Bible says that God commands His angels to guard you in all of your ways. That means you are surrounded by angels who were put there to protect you. You might not be able to see them, but they are standing guard even now. Wow, what an amazing thought!

God cares enough about you that He wants to protect you. He's given His angels charge over you, so rest easy! They've got you covered.

Thank You for giving me guardian angels, Lord! I'm safe in their care. Amen.

DAY 282

HE PROVIDES WHAT WE NEED

The people of Israel called the bread manna. It was white like coriander seed and tasted like wafers made with honey.
Exodus 16:31 NIV

When the Israelites were wandering around in the desert on their way to the Promised Land, they got really hungry. Moses didn't know what to do about that. There were thousands of people to feed and he didn't have any food with him.

Moses didn't need to worry. God had a plan. He sent manna from heaven. "What is manna?" you ask. It's a special type of sweet, tasty bread that fell from the skies. The Israelites ate it every day as they traveled and it filled their stomachs for the journey. (Wow! Can you imagine watching bread falling from the skies?)

God knew the Israelites needed food. He knows what you need too. When you are faithful to ask, He is faithful to provide. What a wonderful God we serve.

Thank You for meeting all of my needs, God. You take such good care of me and my family. Amen.

DAY 283

ENCOURAGING WORDS

Timothy, my son, I am giving you this command in keeping with the prophecies once made about you, so that by recalling them you may fight the battle well.

1 Timothy 1:18 NIV

Sometimes people say nice things about you when you're young and you remember them as you grow up. Maybe someone once said, "You're so smart!" or maybe someone said, "I really love the way you sing. I bet you'll lead worship one day!"

When people say nice things about you, you remember them. Their words give you confidence.

Today's Bible verse is about a young man named Timothy. Many wonderful things were spoken over him when he was a boy, and these words gave him courage as he grew older. He became a missionary and traveled from place to place telling others about Jesus.

What kind words have been spoken over you? Never forget that God has amazing things for you to do. Keep those sweet words in mind as you grow up, and watch as the Lord brings them to pass.

Thank You for the kind words people have spoken over me, Lord. I will remember them as I grow up. Amen.

DAY 284

THE DAY JESUS DIED

Jesus carried His own cross to a hill called the Place of the Skull. There they nailed Him to the cross. With Him were two others. There was one on each side of Jesus.
John 19:17–18

Maybe you've heard the story about how Jesus died for you and took away all your sins. That was a very sad day. His accusers made Him carry His own cross all the way up the hill, and when He reached the top they nailed Him to the cross and crucified (killed) Him.

You will have to do a lot of brave things in your life, but you will never have to do anything as brave as what Jesus did that day. He laid down His life so that you could have life. He washed away your sins so that you could be forgiven.

If you've ever wondered what Jesus was thinking about as He carried that cross, here's the answer—He was thinking of you.

Jesus, You were thinking of me? I didn't know that! You did it all for me, Lord, and I am so grateful. Thank You for being so brave and so loving. Amen.

DAY 285

HE MEETS YOUR NEEDS

And my God will give you everything you need because of His great riches in Christ Jesus.
PHILIPPIANS 4:19

If someone asked you to make a list of all of the things you need, what would be first on the list? What would be second or third? Would you really list only the things you needed, or would your list include things you want as well? There's a difference between the two, you know.

Today's verse is a promise from the Bible that God will meet all of your needs. He's going to make sure you have everything you need to survive: a place to live, a place to sleep, food to eat, water to drink, people to love, and someone to take care of you. These are the most basic needs you will have in life.

God will never let you down. He's looking out for you, ready to take care of you like a good father would. You are His child, after all.

Thank You for meeting my needs, Lord. I will never go without because You love me and take care of me. Amen.

DAY 286

DON'T COMPARE

We do not compare ourselves with those who think they are good. They compare themselves with themselves. They decide what they think is good or bad and compare themselves with those ideas. They are foolish.

2 Corinthians 10:12

Do you ever play the comparison game? Maybe you compare your hair to someone else's. Or maybe you compare your clothes to what the girls in your class are wearing. Maybe you compare your talents and abilities to a friend who is super talented. When you make these comparisons, you feel like you're not as good as the others.

God never meant for us to compare ourselves to others. The only opinion that matters is His. There will always be people who are better at some things than you are, and there will always be people who are not quite as good at those things. That's just how life is.

When you compare, it's easy to get jealous or bitter. God doesn't want that. He only wants you to celebrate the gifts He has placed inside of you and not compare them with anyone else's.

I get it, Lord. No comparing.
I will do my best from now on. Amen.

DAY 287

BESTIES

What can we say about all these things?
Since God is for us, who can be against us?
ROMANS 8:31

Not everyone is going to want to be your friend. In fact, some people probably won't be friendly to you at all. . .and that's okay. Not everyone is meant to be a bestie.

Maybe you don't feel like you have any friends at all, at least none who truly care. Perhaps it feels like everyone is against you and no one is for you. Maybe you're a little jealous of the kids who hang out with their friends. You wonder if you'll ever know what that feels like.

Today's verse is all the proof you will ever need that someone wants to be your friend. *God* is for you, so who can be against you? It doesn't matter how many people don't seem to like you—the Creator of the universe adores you and calls you His own. He will always be on your side, for you are His precious daughter. Now that's a true bestie!

Thank You for being on my side, Lord! You are such an amazing friend, and I love You so much. Amen.

DAY 288

HIS WAYS ARE HIGHER

"For My thoughts are not your thoughts, and My ways are not your ways," says the Lord. "For as the heavens are higher than the earth, so are My ways higher than your ways, and My thoughts than your thoughts."

Isaiah 55:8–9

Even if you try your entire life, you will never be able to figure God out. He is so far above us that we simply cannot understand how His mind works.

Think about the most brilliant person you know. God is ten million times more brilliant than that. He thinks about things that we can't even imagine. He performs miracles that we could never even describe. He loves in a way that is deeper and wider than any human love we will ever experience.

The more you spend time with the Lord in prayer and Bible study, the more you will see that He is truly amazing in every single way. Isn't it remarkable to realize that this brilliant God and Creator of all would take the time to think about you?

You are so amazing, Lord, and yet You love me. I'm so grateful. Amen.

DAY 289

CHOOSE TO SERVE HIM

"If you think it is wrong to serve the Lord, choose today whom you will serve. Choose the gods your fathers worshiped on the other side of the river, or choose the gods of the Amorites in whose land you are living. But as for me and my family, we will serve the Lord."

JOSHUA 24:15

Not everyone in this world wants to follow Jesus. Not everyone wants to be saved. Many people choose to disobey God and turn their back on Him. They follow the gods of this world, or they claim there is no god at all.

Even if everyone around you decides *not* to follow Jesus, you should still follow Him. You make His heart happy when you stand up for what you believe.

Read this verse from Joshua and you will see that God wants you to choose to be on His team. He wants you to choose to serve Him, even if no one else will. It takes courage to live this way. Will you be courageous and take a stand for God even if others do not?

Lord, I will stand for You! I will choose to walk with You every day of my life, no matter what. Amen.

DAY 290

WITH ALL YOUR HEART

Whatever work you do, do it with all your heart.
Do it for the Lord and not for men.
COLOSSIANS 3:23

Have you ever heard the term *half-hearted*? To do something half-heartedly means you don't give it all of your energy. You slack off. You're a little, well, lazy.

Here's an example: Mom wants you to clean up the toys in the playroom. You don't really feel like doing it, so you move very s-l-o-w-l-y, like a snail. You don't give it your best effort. In fact, you're hardly giving it any effort at all!

Half an hour later the room still looks like a mess because you're barely working. Mom comes in and says, "What in the world were you doing in here?" You just shrug because, after all, you weren't doing much.

God wants you to work with your whole heart. He wants you to perform every task as if you were doing it for Him. You will get the work done sooner and feel much better about what you have accomplished.

Lord, I will work hard for You! I will dive in and work with my whole heart. Amen.

DAY 291

THINK BEFORE YOU SPEAK

He who is careful in what he says has much learning, and he who has a quiet spirit is a man of understanding.
PROVERBS 17:27

Your mom just told you to do the dishes, but it's your sister's turn, not yours. You feel like smarting off to your mom. Instead, you close your mouth and count to three very slowly. You release a breath and then respond kindly.

Your father just blamed you for making your brother cry. You start to throw a fit and explain *why* you were fighting with your brother, but then you close your mouth, count to three, and take a slow breath.

Thinking before you speak is always a good idea, in good situations and bad. When you choose a thoughtful response, you're less likely to get into trouble. You're also less likely to say something you'll regret.

Think about the last time you said the wrong thing. Don't you wish you'd taken the time to think before saying it?

Lord, I will think before I speak. I won't spout off in anger. Help me, please! Amen.

DAY 292

GOODBYE, BROKEN HEART!

"God will take away all their tears.
There will be no more death or sorrow or crying or pain. All the old things have passed away."
REVELATION 21:4

Have you ever watched someone else cry? It's really sad, isn't it? Maybe you witnessed one of your parents crying after someone they loved passed away. Or maybe you saw one of the kids at school crying because someone hurt her feelings.

It's so hard to see a loved one suffer a broken heart. Maybe you have been brokenhearted a time or two yourself, so you understand. It hurts!

Here's some good news from the Word of God: The Bible says that when we get to heaven there will be no more tears, no more crying. In heaven everything will be wonderful. There will be no broken hearts. There will be no death. We will leave all of the hard things behind us and live a true "happily ever after" with Jesus.

I can't wait to see what heaven is going to be like, Lord. Thank You for taking away our sadness. Amen.

DAY 293

HUMBLE YOURSELF

Let another man praise you, and not your own mouth. Let a stranger, and not your own lips.
Proverbs 27:2

Have you ever heard the expression "She toots her own horn"? It means someone brags about herself. . .a lot.

Maybe you've hung out with people like this. They're always telling you about the amazing things they've done—how great their grades are, the latest, greatest gaming system they got, how talented they think they are, and so on.

Braggers are hard to be around. They wear you out!

Are you a bragger? Do you talk about yourself a lot? If so, it's time to put a clamp on it. The Bible says you should let others praise you, not sing your own praises. God wants you to be humble and meek, never bragging about yourself. It's hard to do, but it's the right way to live.

**Lord, I don't want to be a bragger.
Please help me focus on lifting others up instead. Amen.**

DAY 294

POWER FROM THE HOLY SPIRIT

"But you will receive power when the Holy Spirit comes into your life. You will tell about Me in the city of Jerusalem and over all the countries of Judea and Samaria and to the ends of the earth."
Acts 1:8

Did you know that you are a missionary? It's true! God might not be calling you to live in Africa or to travel to Central America to share the gospel, but He is asking you to share your faith wherever you happen to be—at your school, in your neighborhood, even on the playground.

Where do you get the courage to share your faith? It comes from the Holy Spirit who lives inside of you. When you are weak, He is strong. When you are timid, He is bold. When you say, "I can't!" He says, "I can!"

The next time you feel like sharing your faith with someone, don't be scared. Just say, "Holy Spirit, speak through me!" and He will do it. He will give you power to share all that Jesus has done in your life.

Holy Spirit, thank You for living inside of me and giving me power. I'm bolder because of You! Amen.

DAY 295

GOD, OUR HELPER

God is our safe place and our strength.
He is always our help when we are in trouble.
Psalm 46:1

Have you ever been in a tough situation where you had to scream, "Help!" If so, who came running? Your mom? Your dad? A teacher? You probably felt so much better when they arrived to help you, right? Your courage was boosted when the adult showed up!

It's good to call on the adults in your life of course, but don't forget to call on God too. He wants you to know that He is your very best helper. When you're in a real jam, you can call out to Him. Say, "God, please help!" He shows up in a hurry!

The Bible says that God is our safe place. Whenever you're hurting or feeling sad, remember you can always run to Him. He loves to hear what you're going through. Aren't you glad the Lord is your helper and friend?

Thank You for being my safe place, God.
I'm so glad You are there for me when I need help!
I will call out to You when I'm sad or hurting. Amen.

DAY 296

SET FREE!

About midnight Paul and Silas were praying and singing songs of thanks to God. The other men in prison were listening to them.
Acts 16:25

Paul and Silas were two amazing missionaries who traveled from place to place telling others about Jesus. They risked their lives to share the gospel.

One time, they were arrested and thrown in prison for sharing their faith. Can you even imagine? But a crazy thing happened! They began to sing and pray very loudly when all of a sudden, an earthquake shook the prison and the prison doors flew open. Their chains fell off!

Wow! God really protected them, didn't He?

Have you ever shared your faith with someone else? It's not always easy, but it's always the right thing to do. Don't be afraid! God will be right there to guard and protect you as you share what He has done for you.

What a cool story, Lord! When Paul and Silas prayed and sang, You saved them. You set them free from prison. I want to be just as courageous! Amen.

DAY 297

BE A DIFFERENCE MAKER

Do not trouble yourself because of sinful men.
Do not want to be like those who do wrong.
Psalm 37:1

Do you get really upset every time kids at school act up? Do you feel irritated when they disobey? Do you get mad when they get away with doing wrong things?

The Bible says you shouldn't spend too much time fretting over the things that sinful people do. Don't get caught up in the drama. Don't become part of the gossip train.

You need to stay focused on making sure *you* are living a holy life. People will realize there's something special about you. You live a different sort of life. You refuse to disobey.

Others are curious about why you're different, so you tell them about Jesus. You share about the difference He has made in your life. Before long, more and more kids are hanging out with you, wanting to know Him too.

Lord, I get it. I need to stay away from the drama. When kids disobey and act up, I'll stay out of it. I'll go on shining my light from a distance. Help me, I pray. Amen.

DAY 298

THE STARING GAME

You will keep the man in perfect peace whose mind is kept on You, because he trusts in You.

Isaiah 26:3

Have you ever played the staring game? You stare into a friend's eyes and do your best not to blink. The first one who blinks loses.

God wants you to keep your eyes on Him. Stay focused on Him and on His Word, and you will be successful. Keep your trust in Him, keep your thoughts on Him, and you will bring joy to His heart. It's kind of like the staring game, but you're allowed to blink!

It's not always easy to stay focused, though. Life is filled with distractions. Ask the Lord to help you keep your focus on Him, even when things around you are going crazy. You can do it!

Please help me to keep my eyes on You, Lord! I will keep reading my Bible, keep praying, and stay focused, even when things around me are swirling! Amen.

DAY 299

A SPECIAL TIME

There is a special time for everything.
There is a time for everything that happens
under heaven. There is a time to be
born, and a time to die; a time to plant,
and a time to pick what is planted.
ECCLESIASTES 3:1–2

The Bible says there's a special time (a season) for everything. If you live on a farm, you already know this! There's planting season and harvest season. You put the seeds in the ground during planting season, and the fruits and veggies are ready to be picked during harvest season.

Just like that farm, you will go through different seasons in your life. During harvest-type seasons, God will use you in mighty ways. During planting-type seasons, things might be quieter. You'll go through fun seasons, sad seasons, busy seasons, calm seasons.

Remember, seasons don't last forever. If you're not happy with the season you're in right now, don't worry! Another one is just around the corner!

Lord, I've been through so many different seasons in my life already, and I want to trust You through all of them. Amen.

DAY 300

THE WORDS OF THE WISE

The words of the wise heard in quiet are better than the loud words of a ruler among fools.
Ecclesiastes 9:17

Some people just love to be heard. They share their opinion (loudly) with everyone they meet. They always think they're right as they *yak-yak-yak* at the top of their lungs.

These people are hard to be around because they act like know-it-alls. God's Word says that it's better for wise words to be spoken in quiet than for foolish words to be shouted. Those know-it-alls don't always win in the end. People don't like to hang around pushy people for long, do they?

What about you? Do you speak wise words in quiet, or do you shout like a know-it-all? It's time to examine how you speak to others. Calm, quiet words will do the trick. Loud, proud words will drive people away.

Lord, I don't want to be a know-it-all. I won't show off or demand my own way. I'll guard my tongue and speak quiet, kind words. Amen.

DAY 301

HE GIVES GOOD GIFTS

Whatever is good and perfect comes to us from God. He is the One Who made all light. He does not change. No shadow is made by His turning.
JAMES 1:17

Think about the most talented person you know. Maybe she's an amazing singer. Now think about some other talents your friends have. Maybe some of them are good at ballet. Maybe others are really good at playing sports or painting pictures. Some kids are great in school and always make good grades. If you look around you, you'll see a lot of amazing gifts out there!

Every talent, every gift, comes from God. That means the girl with the beautiful singing voice is anointed by God to sing. The girl who is a beautiful dancer is gifted by God to dance. It's amazing to think that He gives such good gifts to His children, isn't it?

What gifts has God given you? Are you using them for Him? Remember, He's given you those gifts for a reason!

Lord, thank You for giving us such good gifts. I want to use my gifts for You so that others can see Your goodness. Amen.

DAY 302

THANK GOD FOR YOUR CHRISTIAN FRIENDS

We must give thanks to God for you always, Christian brothers. It is the right thing to do because your faith is growing so much. Your love for each other is stronger all the time.
2 Thessalonians 1:3

Do you have any Christian friends at school or in your neighborhood? Do you have friends at church? If so, you need to thank God for them.

Having a friend who believes the way you do is so important. She can encourage you in your faith and help you grow.

Take a look at today's verse. The Bible says we are always to give thanks for our friends. How often? Always. Why? Because they provide us with spiritual nutrition. They keep us strong. They also help us when we do the wrong things. These godly friends pick us up, brush us off, and say, "Keep going! You can do this!"

Where would we be without our godly friends?

Thank You for my Christian friends, Lord.
I love them and am so grateful for them. Amen.

DAY 303

A LEADER LIKE MOSES

Moses said to the Lord, "Lord, I am not a man of words. I have never been. Even now since You spoke to Your servant, I still am not. For I am slow in talking and it is difficult for me to speak."
EXODUS 4:10

The Israelites had lived as slaves in Egypt for a long, long time. When the time came for them to leave Egypt and go to the Promised Land, God knew they would need a leader. He chose a man named Moses.

Moses didn't think he would make a good leader. In fact, he was pretty sure he would be the worst possible leader. He had a problem with his speech. He stuttered. He didn't feel he was up for the job.

Can you relate to Moses? Maybe you've thought, *I'm not right for this job! The teacher needs to pick someone else.*

The truth is, you can do all things through Jesus Christ who gives you strength (Philippians 4:13). Like Moses, you can do far beyond what you even imagine. Don't give up before you start. Just think of Moses leading all those people to the Promised Land.

Lord, thank You for choosing me.

DAY 304

WHITE AS SNOW

But Christ has brought you back to God by His death on the cross. In this way, Christ can bring you to God, holy and pure and without blame.
COLOSSIANS 1:22

Imagine you went outside to play in a mud puddle. You splashed up and down until your shoes and your legs were covered in mud. Before long, your clothes were muddy too.

In some ways, that's what it's like when you come to Jesus for the first time. It's like you're covered in mud, a dirty mess. Instead of scolding you, He looks at you and says, "Let Me clean that up!"

How does Jesus clean you up? When He died on the cross, His blood washed away all of your sins. You just have to believe in your heart that He died for you and ask Him to come and live in your life. Make Him your Lord and Savior. Then you will be fully clean, white as snow. No more mud on you, girl!

Thank You, Lord, for cleaning me up. I've made some real messes over the years, but You have washed me white as snow.

DAY 305

HEAD OVER ALL

When you have Christ, you are complete.
He is the head over all leaders and powers.
COLOSSIANS 2:10

Imagine you are the queen of a make-believe country. All of your people have to obey the laws you set. You watch over them carefully, making sure they obey you. But who do *you* obey? Who is your leader if you're the queen?

Now imagine you're the president of the United States. You have a lot of power, don't you? You get to help pass laws and tell other people how to live. But who tells *you* how to live?

Jesus Christ is the Ruler of all rulers. He's the King of all kings. You could say He's the President of all presidents. Every human being has to bow to Him, even the really important ones like kings and queens. He is the head of them all. What an amazing leader our God is!

God, You are King of kings and Lord of lords.
You are above all, and I worship You! Amen.

DAY 306

LIKE A LION

The sinful run away when no one is trying to catch them, but those who are right with God have as much strength of heart as a lion.
PROVERBS 28:1

Think about a lion. What pops into your mind? A big cat? Maybe he's taking a nap under a tree with nothing to worry about. Maybe he's chasing his dinner with no fear of being chased himself. Lions are brave and strong. The Bible compares God's kids to lions. But sometimes, don't you feel more like a scrawny rabbit than a strong lion? Something scary happens, and you want to hop, hop away as fast as you can.

With God, though, you don't have to fear. That's because Jesus, the lion, has saved us from every fear—the littlest to the biggest. Revelation 5:5 tells us, "Stop crying. See! The Lion from the family group of Judah has power and has won." That same lion's Spirit is inside you now. When something scary happens, trust Him to make you as brave and strong as a lion.

Jesus, thank You that I don't have to be courageous on my own. Please give me Your courage today. Amen.

DAY 307

ALWAYS THERE

"Be strong and have strength of heart. . . . For the Lord your God is the One Who goes with you. He will be faithful to you. He will not leave you alone."
DEUTERONOMY 31:6

Let's say it's the first day of school and it's lunchtime. You walk into the cafeteria and your feet slow down, then stop. You look from table to table. Your heart starts jogging in your chest as you search for a place to sit, and you begin to wonder what you'll do if you *can't* find a place to sit. . .and then you see her! Your friend, waving to you. Yes, seeing a friend when you feel scared and alone is the best thing in the world.

Just think. No matter where you go—even to a brand-new place with no friends—you are not alone. God is faithful; He will always be there. And He isn't just a friend you see once you get somewhere. He walks into every situation right beside you.

God, thanks for being my friend. Help me remember that You will never leave me by myself. Amen.

DAY 308

NEED A BOOST?

When the Christians heard of our coming, they came to meet us. They came as far as the town of Appius and to a place to stay called the Three Stores. When Paul saw them, he thanked God and took courage.

Acts 28:15

Ever had a bad day? Or a bunch of bad days? Well, Paul, a follower of God, was having some bad months. First he was put in prison for doing nothing wrong. Then on the long voyage to Rome for his trial, he battled a fierce storm at sea and was shipwrecked. But once he *finally* made it to Rome, the Christians welcomed him. The Bible says that Paul "thanked God and took courage" as soon as he saw them. He felt a boost of courage knowing he had the support of friends.

You can be like those early Christians who encouraged Paul. You don't need to say something special. You don't really need to *do* anything. Just be present. Just let others see that they have a friend.

Jesus, You give me so much courage. Use me to help other people have courage too. Amen.

DAY 309

BOLD STEPS

"Only be strong and have much strength of heart. Be careful to obey all the Law which My servant Moses told you. Do not turn from it to the right or to the left. Then all will go well with you everywhere you go."

JOSHUA 1:7

Some people obey God because they are afraid of Him. They don't want to be punished, so they try very hard to do everything right. If you've asked God to forgive your sins, you don't need to fear His punishment. . .so why is obedience still important?

We should obey God for lots of reasons, but one reason is that obedience gives us courage. God loves us so much, and everything He tells us is meant to protect us and to show us how to be like Him. When we use His words to guide our steps, we won't wander into trouble the way we would if we chose our own way to go. We can know *for sure* that following His way is the best way. So live courageously. God won't lead you down the wrong path.

God, I'm following You—courageously! Amen.

DAY 310

TELL ME AGAIN

"Have I not told you? Be strong and have strength of heart! Do not be afraid or lose faith. For the Lord your God is with you anywhere you go."

JOSHUA 1:9

God had a big job for Joshua. Joshua would be Israel's next leader after Moses, the man God chose to lead His people out of Egypt and to whom God gave His commandments on Mount Sinai. God knew Joshua could do what He asked because He would be with Joshua. But God also knew that Joshua would need a big dose of courage, as big as the big job. So when God told Joshua what to do, He also told Joshua to be courageous. . .three times!

Sometimes we need reassurance—words that help us not to be scared—so we can be brave. Sometimes we need to hear those words again and again. If you need a dose of courage, listen for God's voice in your heart. Hear Him say, "Be courageous! Because I am with you everywhere."

God, I'm not feeling very brave.
Please remind me what Your Word says. Amen.

"I have taken you from the ends of the earth. I have called you from its farthest parts. . . . Do not fear, for I am with you. Do not be afraid, for I am your God. I will give you strength, and for sure I will help you. Yes, I will hold you up with My right hand that is right and good."

ISAIAH 41:9–10

If you read the Bible from cover to cover, you'll probably notice that God tells His people not to fear, and He tells them that a lot. But whenever God tells us, "Don't be afraid," He never says, "Because you're so awesome." We can be fearless because *He's* so awesome! Look again at the verses from Isaiah. Count the number of times God uses *I* to describe what He does to take care of His people: "*I* have taken"; "*I* have called"; "*I* am with you"; "*I* am your God"; "*I* will give"; "*I* with help"; "*I* will hold."

So. . .want to become more courageous? Shift your focus from you to Him.

God, thank You for everything You do! Amen.

DAY 312

TOUGH TO OBEY

Then Barak said to her, "I will go if you go with me. But if you do not go with me, I will not go." And she said, "For sure I will go with you. But the honor will not be yours as you go on your way. . . ." Then Deborah got up and went with Barak to Kedesh.

Judges 4:8–9

Both Deborah and Barak knew that God had commanded Barak to lead an army to fight King Jabin. But Barak was afraid to go, while Deborah had the courage to trust God.

At times you might feel like Deborah just a tiny bit. Maybe you and your friends know what God says about something, but your friends are afraid that if they obey God, other kids will make fun of them. Or maybe obeying God means missing out on what other kids are doing. Trust God in situations like this. Be courageous even when others aren't, and you might help them be courageous too!

God, obeying You isn't always easy, but I want to be courageous no matter what. Amen.

DAY 313

STEP RIGHT UP!

We can come to God without fear because
we have put our trust in Christ.
EPHESIANS 3:12

We use a lot of words to describe God: *awesome*, *mighty*, *perfect*, *holy*, *most high*, *all-powerful*, just to list a few! God is a *big* God. We can't even know everything about Him—He's too big for our minds to understand. Then there's us. We could use a lot of words to describe ourselves: *ordinary*, *weak*, *imperfect*, *sinful*, *low*, *powerless*. . . Yikes! We're so little compared to God's bigness. Shouldn't we be scared to come to Him?

Not if we believe in His Son, Jesus Christ! Because Jesus died for our sins, we can be fearless. Because of Jesus, the almighty God is also our heavenly Father. And we never need to be scared to come to our Father. He loves us. Remember how *big* God is? Well, His love is that big too.

God, my Father, I'm so happy that You love me so much and that I can come right up next to You. You are awesome! Amen.

DAY 314

COURAGEOUS FAITH

Jesus said to him, "Why do you ask Me that? The one who has faith can do all things." At once the father cried out. He said with tears in his eyes, "Lord, I have faith. Help my weak faith to be stronger!"
MARK 9:23–24

Talk about dramatic! The scene could be from a movie—but it really happened. A big crowd had gathered because Jesus' disciples could not cast out a demon from a boy. While the people argued, Jesus surprised them by showing up. They brought the boy to Him, and quicker than you can blink, the demon caused the boy to fall down and roll around and foam at the mouth. That's when the boy's father asked Jesus to help *if* He could. But there are no ifs with God! Jesus told the man that *anything* is possible with faith.

How would you have responded? The boy's father cried out for Jesus to help his faith grow stronger. . .and you can do that too.

Lord, when I'm scared, I don't always believe that You can do impossible things. Help me have more faith! Amen.

DAY 315

ARE YOU WILLING?

Then Mary said, "I am willing to be used of the Lord. Let it happen to me as you have said." Then the angel went away from her.
LUKE 1:38

The Bible doesn't tell us much about Mary, but we can see that she was courageous. Her life would be very different after the angel Gabriel visited her with some huge news. God had chosen her to give birth to God's Son, Jesus! Mary probably didn't understand everything. (How would the Holy Spirit form the child inside her, and when?) She probably had only begun to think about how her life would change. (Would she be called names? Would Joseph still marry her?) But she said, "I'm willing," and let God handle the rest.

Sometimes being courageous means allowing God to work in us when we don't understand. It means saying yes to Him when His will might require us to go through difficult things. But He will be with you every moment, so be courageous, girl!

God, I want to be like Mary. Use me in whatever ways You want to! Amen.

DAY 316

#1

"First of all, look for the holy nation of God. Be right with Him. All these other things will be given to you also."
MATTHEW 6:33

What things grab your attention throughout the day? School, sports, homework, chores? Pets, screens, hobbies, friends? It doesn't matter how old you are, this world is full of distractions—things that pull our attention from what we should be thinking about most. Even in Bible days, people thought a lot about earthly things—what they would wear and what they would eat—and not so much about heaven. But Jesus told them to flip that mindset, and He's still telling us today. "*First* seek God," He says. Then the rest will fall into place.

Seeking God first might mean reading your Bible before watching TV. It might mean spending time praying before chatting with your friends. You'll need courage to put godly things first when there are so many other things you could put first instead. So ask God to help. He will!

God, please help me think about You first. Amen.

DAY 317

HATERS

Do not be afraid of those who hate you.
Their hate for you proves they will be destroyed.
It proves you have life from God that lasts forever.
PHILIPPIANS 1:28

Being a Jesus follower at church in a room full of your friends is fun, isn't it? But what about at your school or in your city? We're not always surrounded by people who believe what we do, and that can be tough. The sad truth is that Christians aren't always treated kindly. This verse tells us to be brave despite how other people feel about us. Their hate shouldn't make us tremble. Why not? Because God promises that He will win and that we will live forever. He holds our future (and us) steady.

So keep telling other people about God. Keep letting them see Jesus by living the way He lived. Be courageous! The Bible says that God doesn't want anyone to be unsaved (1 Timothy 2:4), and He just might use you to lead someone to Him.

God, I feel bad when people don't like me.
Help me bravely follow You anyway. Amen.

DAY 318

PERFECT TIMING

"Do not worry about tomorrow. . . .
The troubles we have in a day are enough for one day."
MATTHEW 6:34

Corrie ten Boom lived during World War II. She hid Jews in her home to protect them from the Nazis even though doing that was very dangerous. Pretty brave, huh? But as a young girl, Corrie didn't think she would ever have the strength to do something brave—like even die!—for Jesus. She asked her father about this, and he told her to think about a train trip and when he would give her the money to buy her ticket. Weeks before? No! He would give her the money just before she got on the train. And God, our heavenly Father, does the same thing when we need courage. We may wonder why He doesn't give us all we'll ever need *right now*. But Jesus tells us, "Don't worry about the future. Live each day one by one." And God will give us courage *right when we need it.*

God, You know everything I'll need every day.
Thank You that I can count on You. Amen.

DAY 319

PRAY!

Let us go with complete trust to the throne of God. We will receive His loving-kindness and have His loving-favor to help us whenever we need it.
HEBREWS 4:16

Some people pray only when they go to church. Some people pray only when something bad happens. Some people pray only about big things. . . Did you know that we can pray about everything, all the time? In fact, the Bible says to "never stop praying" (1 Thessalonians 5:17).

But sometimes you might feel shy about talking to God. Have you ever thought, *What if I sin and God won't listen to me anymore? What if my prayer is about something really tiny and God doesn't care? What if I've already prayed about something a lot and God is annoyed?* God doesn't want us to be timid about prayer. We can be bold! We can go to God totally confident that He will respond with loving-kindness and loving-favor. "Ask," Jesus said (Matthew 7:7). So go ahead. Talk to Him!

Lord, I never have to be afraid to talk to You. Thank You for hearing everything I say. Amen.

DAY 320

SET FREE

I want to do good but I do not. I do not do the good I want to do. . . . Who can set me free from my sinful old self?
ROMANS 7:18–19, 24

Your mom tells you to clean your room. But your room is *so* messy that you pretend you didn't hear her. That girl in your class is saying mean things again. You know you should be nice to her, but you say mean things back. Your teacher asks why you don't have your homework, and you make up a story. Well, the story was kind of true, so it's not a lie, right?

Obeying God is tough! And no matter how hard you try and how much you want to obey, sometimes you will sin. Paul, the man who wrote these verses from Romans, learned that sometimes he sinned even when he didn't want to. He also learned that Jesus could set him free. It might take some courage to tell God your mistakes. But He forgives. He saves us from sin! And He will help us obey.

Jesus, thank You for saving me. I hate when I do wrong things. . .please help me! Amen.

DAY 321

LIKE JESUS

Do not act like the sinful people of the world. Let God change your life. First of all, let Him give you a new mind. Then you will know what God wants you to do.
ROMANS 12:2

Most of us match our behavior to someone else—we try to be like other people by acting like them, talking like them, or looking like them. Maybe your model is an older sibling, your friends, or a favorite celebrity.

As Christians, our model should be Christ. So how do we become like Him? To be Christlike, we have to be Christ-minded. Let God change the way you think first so you'll know how to act. The best way to let God change your thinking is to read the Bible. But be ready. Being more and more like Jesus means being less and less like the world. You will be different, and it takes courage to be different. Isn't it great that Jesus is full of courage—and you'll be like Him in that way too!

Jesus, give me a new mind as I read the Bible. I want to be like You. Amen.

DAY 322

READY TO GO

Then I heard the voice of the Lord, saying, "Whom should I send? Who will go for Us?" Then I said, "Here am I. Send me!"

Isaiah 6:8

God has chosen ordinary people to do extraordinary things for Him. A lot of these ordinary people didn't think they could do those extraordinary things. Moses asked God to choose someone else (Exodus 4:13). He was bad at public speaking—how could he talk to Pharaoh? Gideon questioned God's choice too (Judges 6:15). After all, Gideon was the little guy in the weakest family—how could he win battles?

What about Isaiah? Isaiah might have wondered why God chose him. His first words after seeing a vision of the Lord were "It is bad for me, for I am destroyed!" (Isaiah 6:5). Isaiah knew he was a sinner and not worthy to be near God. But when God asked who would go to the people with a message, Isaiah raised his hand. Isaiah trusted God to make him ready, and so he courageously said, "Here am I. Send me!"

God, I'm only me, but please use me to do extraordinary things. Amen.

DAY 323

STORMY

Jesus and His followers got into a boat. Jesus said to them, "Let us go over to the other side of the lake." Then they pushed out into the water. As they were going, Jesus fell asleep. A wind storm came over the lake. The boat was filling with water and they were in danger. The followers came to awake Jesus. They said, "Teacher! Teacher! We are going to die!" Then Jesus got up and spoke sharp words to the wind and the high waves. The wind stopped blowing and there were no more waves. He said to them, "Where is your faith?"

LUKE 8:22–25

As you grow up, you might hear people talk about the "storms" of life. Everybody—including kids—goes through hard things. But we can have courage when troubles seem to hit us like waves crashing into a boat—because Jesus is in the boat with us! Jesus' followers didn't look for Jesus until they were terrified. They were too busy looking at the storm! Instead, keep your thoughts on Jesus, the one who can calm any storm!

Jesus, I'm not afraid, because I know You are here. Amen.

DAY 324

MEGA FORGIVENESS

While they threw stones at Stephen, he prayed, "Lord Jesus, receive my spirit." After that he fell on his knees and cried out with a loud voice, "Lord, do not hold this sin against them."
Acts 7:59–60

God expects us to forgive people just as He forgives us. But what about when people do mean things? Like, really mean things. Should we forgive them? Should we want God to forgive them?

Stephen, an early Christian, was martyred for his faith—he was killed for believing in Jesus. Soon after Jesus had come back to life, some people in Jerusalem were upset because Stephen was preaching about Jesus. So they told lies, arrested Stephen, and eventually killed him. But just before he died, Stephen prayed for God to forgive those people! He believed that Jesus died for *every* sin. (Yes, even the cruelest, most horrible sin you can think of.) And Stephen believed that God would make things right. He chose forgiveness. How courageous!

God, give me strength to forgive as courageously as You do. Amen.

DAY 325

INNOCENT!

Love is made perfect in us when we are not ashamed as we stand before Him on the day He judges. For we know that our life in this world is His life lived in us. . . . Perfect love puts fear out of our hearts.

1 John 4:17–18

Have you ever seen a courtroom trial? When the person stands in front of the judge to hear the judge's decision, they usually look nervous. That's because the judge will say whether they are guilty or innocent—whether they will be punished or go free. God, the ultimate judge, will judge all people one day. But we don't need to fear that day. Here's why:

Even though we're sinners—we're guilty and deserve punishment—God loves us and sent Jesus to live a sinless life and take our punishment for us. We're forgiven when we believe in Jesus, and it's as if His life becomes our own. There's no fear in our hearts when we stand before God because He sees Jesus' innocence—and we go free!

Lord, thank You for Your love and for Jesus! Amen.

DAY 326

DREAMERS

Then he had another dream. . . . He said, "I have had another dream. The sun and the moon and eleven stars were bowing down to me." He told it to his father and to his brothers. His father spoke sharp words to him, saying, "What is this dream you have had? Will I and your mother and brothers come to bow ourselves down to the ground in front of you?" Joseph's brothers were jealous of him. But his father thought about what he said.

GENESIS 37:9–11

Joseph's dream sure caused a lot of hoopla. His father scolded him but then began to wonder about the dream. Joseph's brothers, who already hated him, were jealous and threw him into a pit to get even. What did Joseph think about his dream? The Bible doesn't say, but Joseph stayed close to God and trusted Him to unfold His plans. If God gives you a dream, some people may not respond positively. They may laugh or doubt or be jealous. Trust God anyway. Have courage to believe in God's dreams for you.

God, I can be brave and trust You even with my dreams. Amen.

DAY 327

[Jesus] said, "I tell you the truth, this poor woman has put in more than all of them. For they have put in a little of the money they had no need for. She is very poor and has put in all she had."

Luke 21:3–4

If you had thousands of dollars and you gave one dollar away, you wouldn't miss it, right? You would have plenty left over. Well, in these verses, a poor woman had only two small coins and she put both in the offering box. Today, that would be like having just one penny—and giving that penny away! Jesus praised her generosity, but He also praised her faith. She had courage to believe that God would provide out of nothing.

Are you courageous enough to give in big ways? And don't limit generosity to money. There are lots of ways to share, like donating your favorite toys or spending a whole Saturday raking leaves for a neighbor. God always gives generously, and so can we.

Lord, You give me everything!
So I want to give as much as I can. Amen.

DAY 328

SHOW 'EM!

Let no one show little respect for you because you are young. Show other Christians how to live by your life. They should be able to follow you in the way you talk and in what you do. Show them how to live in faith and in love and in holy living.

1 Timothy 4:12

Why do kids want to be older? If you're in elementary school, you can't wait to be a middle schooler. And when you're in middle school, you can't wait until high school. It's true that getting older means you can do more things. You get to stay up later, hang out with your friends without parents around, and even drive a car! Sometimes it might seem like you can't do *anything* when you're young—and sometimes adults act like you can't do anything. But that's not what God thinks. You can be an example for others to follow *now*. Don't be discouraged if people treat you like a little kid. Instead, keep living for God, and show others how to live too.

God, make me an example—even for people waaaay older than me! Amen.

DAY 329

KEEP PRACTICING

No person who has become a child of God keeps on sinning. This is because the Holy Spirit is in him. He cannot keep on sinning because God is his Father. . . . The person who does not keep on doing what is right and does not love his brother does not belong to God.

1 John 3:9–10

Have you ever heard someone say, "Practice makes perfect"? A lot of things take practice before you get good at them. Think about playing a guitar or hitting a tennis ball. You have to strum and swing over and over until you get it just right. And while you're at it, you'll make mistakes, but you'll keep practicing so you get better and better.

Living the way God wants us to live takes practice too. We *will* make mistakes; we will sin sometimes. But as with playing an instrument or sport, don't give up! Be brave to learn from your mistakes and to keep trying. With God's Spirit inside you cheering you on, you *will* get better and better!

Holy Spirit, help me practice doing right. Amen.

DAY 330

GREATER THINGS

"For sure, I tell you, whoever puts his trust in Me can do the things I am doing. He will do even greater things than these because I am going to the Father. Whatever you ask in My name, I will do it so the shining-greatness of the Father may be seen in the Son."

John 14:12–13

Jesus did remarkable things while He was on the earth, and His first followers did remarkable things too. Maybe after reading about those remarkable things in the Bible, you've wondered, *I'm just me. What can I do for God?* Jesus promised believers that they would do "even greater things" than He did. They will reach every part of the world with His message and His miracles. . .but those things only happen because of Him. It's God's power that makes "greater things" possible, and it's for God's glory that we do them. So be bold! Put your trust in Jesus. Then watch as He does all kinds of great things through you.

Lord, Your power gives me power.
I want to do so much for You! Amen.

DAY 331

BULLIES

*O man, He has told you what is good.
What does the Lord ask of you but to do
what is fair and to love kindness, and to
walk without pride with your God?*
Micah 6:8

Bully—it's a word we hear a lot lately because bullying is so serious and it happens so much. But is there anything we can do about it? What would God want us to do?

In this verse, the prophet Micah reminds us what God wants from us, and the short list includes doing what is fair and loving kindness. If you see someone being picked on, what is fair and kind? Standing up for the person being picked on. Can you guess what you'll need to do that? Yep! Courage. Don't let fear keep you from helping someone who's hurting. And don't be afraid to ask for help yourself. You're not a tattletale, and you're not wimpy. Bullying is just too big to tackle alone. Let's face it together.

God, help me be a friend to kids who are bullied. Amen.

DAY 332

JUST WAIT

Wait for the Lord. Be strong. Let your heart be strong. Yes, wait for the Lord.
Psalm 27:14

Waiting can be soooo boring. Waiting can be soooo hard to do. Like when the sun is shining but you're stuck in school just waiting for the bell to ring. Or like when the line for the roller coaster stretches miles and you're just waiting for your turn. Sometimes we find ourselves waiting for God too. Have you ever prayed about something, then days—maybe weeks!—go by and you're still waiting for God to answer? We humans want God to do things exactly when we want those things to happen. But we have to remember that God doesn't sense time like we do. "A thousand years in Your eyes are like yesterday when it passes by," the psalmist wrote (Psalm 90:4). And God also sees the big picture—He knows everything from the beginning to the end of time and He's working things out better than we could imagine. So be strong. Wait for Him!

God, waiting is hard! But I'll be strong, and I'll wait for You. Amen.

DAY 333

COURAGE FOR THE MISFITS

He grew up before Him like a young plant,
and like a root out of dry ground. He has no
beautiful body and when we see Him there is no
beauty that we should desire Him. He was hated
and men would have nothing to do with Him.
Isaiah 53:2–3

Are you a Miss Popular or a Miss Shy? Truth is, even if it seems like we have lots of friends, sometimes we can feel awkward—like we're nothing special, like we don't fit in, like nobody wants us around. We may wonder if God understands.

These verses from Isaiah describe Jesus. Now, Jesus is God in human form. He is amazing, awesome! But the way He looked on earth was. . .average. What's more, people didn't like Him at all—and that must have hurt a lot. Jesus understands everything you're going through, including the times you feel like a misfit. So how did *He* stay courageous when He felt rejected and out of place? He stuck close to His Father.

God, thank You that I'll always belong with You. Amen.

DAY 334

GOOD FOR YOU

"What man among you would give his son a stone if he should ask for bread? Or if he asks for a fish, would he give him a snake? You are bad and you know how to give good things to your children. How much more will your Father in heaven give good things to those who ask Him?"

MATTHEW 7:9–11

Can you imagine asking for bread and having someone hand you a stone, or asking for a fish and getting a gross snake instead? Pretty ridiculous, right? Parents sin and make mistakes like everyone else, but even they know what giving good things looks like. As much as we would expect *people* to give good things, we can depend on *God* much more! You can pray to your heavenly Father with confidence. Ask away! God cares about you beyond anything you can imagine. He hears your voice every single time. And He won't hand you anything except what is good for you.

Father, thank You for listening to my prayers and giving me good things. Amen.

DAY 335

NOTHING TO FEAR

So we can say for sure, "The Lord is my Helper.
I am not afraid of anything man can do to me."
HEBREWS 13:6

Sadly, people do violent things, and it's easy to get scared. The absolute scariest thing is death, but if you believe in Jesus, you will live forever in heaven. And there's more. Check out these verses: "We know that God makes all things work together for the good of those who love Him. . . . God knew from the beginning who would put their trust in Him. So He chose them and made them to be like His Son. . . . What can we say about all these things? Since God is for us, who can be against us?" (Romans 8:28–29, 31). Always, always remember: Almighty God is active in your life. He's changing you on the inside, and He's controlling all that goes on in the world. He is your helper each day, and with Him on your side, you have nothing to fear.

God, whatever scary things people do, I can be brave because You are my Savior and helper. Amen.

DAY 336

FOREVER FAITHFUL

If we have no faith, He will still be faithful for He cannot go against what He is.
2 Timothy 2:13

What is a faithful friend? She doesn't say one thing when she means another, right? She doesn't promise to do something only to bail out. She doesn't act like your friend one minute, then the next minute totally abandon you.

God is faithful. You can trust His every word. He will keep His promises, every last one. He is with you and for you every moment. And unlike an earthly friend who may let you down, no matter how faithful she is most of the time, God will never fail you because He is the same 100 percent of the time. He won't change His character, even if a person doesn't believe in Him at all. So what does that mean for you, His kid? When you're afraid, when you have doubts, when you worry. . .whatever's going on, you can go to God and find a faithful friend. Guaranteed.

God, thank You for being faithful and always being there for me. Amen.

DAY 337

HOLY INTERPRETER

But the person who is not a Christian does not understand these words from the Holy Spirit. He thinks they are foolish.
1 Corinthians 2:14

Some things in the Bible are hard to understand. Some things might even seem impossible to believe. Like, what about those stories in the Old Testament that are just plain weird? And can anyone really explain the Trinity—God being three persons yet one God? To people who aren't Christians, the Bible is silly, but don't let their opinion drain your confidence in God or His Word. Remember: God's way of doing things isn't our way. The Bible tells us that He "has chosen what the world calls foolish to shame the wise" (1 Corinthians 1:27). God doesn't choose only the brightest, smartest people to be His kids, because no amount of human wisdom can help us know God. Only God can reveal who He is. Only His Spirit can make sense of those hard to understand, "impossible" to believe things.

Holy Spirit, teach me as I read the Bible.
Even if people think the Bible is silly or out of date,
I want to understand and believe boldly! Amen.

DAY 338

YOU'LL BE HAPPY

Who will hurt you if you do what is right? But even if you suffer for doing what is right, you will be happy. Do not be afraid or troubled by what they may do to make it hard for you.
1 PETER 3:13–14

It's good to be a good kid. If you follow the rules, you'll avoid getting into trouble. And people don't usually mistreat others for doing kind things and trying to get along. But the Bible never promises that we won't suffer for doing what is right. It does promise that we'll be happy if we do suffer. Yes, happy! You probably won't be happy about the suffering part, but you will be happy knowing that God is pleased when you obey Him.

Some Bible translations use the word *blessed* instead of *happy*. Remember, God sees everything that goes on in your life. He won't miss your obedience but will bless you for it.

God, You're watching over me always. I'm not going to be scared thinking about what might happen. I'll just keep doing what is right. Amen.

DAY 339

SPEAK UP!

"For if you keep quiet at this time, help will come to the Jews from another place. . . . Who knows if you have not become queen for such a time as this?"
ESTHER 4:14

Speaking up isn't easy. Just ask Queen Esther! Her situation was especially difficult. She had just learned about a plot to destroy the Jews, and her cousin Mordecai wanted her to beg the king to save them. There was only one problem: A person could be killed for entering the king's court without an invitation! Despite what must have been a major case of butterflies in the stomach, Esther listened to Mordecai and went to the king. She didn't know it herself, but she *had* become queen for exactly that time.

It takes courage to speak up, even when opening your mouth won't put you in danger. Maybe a friend is disobeying God and you want to say something to her. Maybe a classmate needs to hear some kind words. Maybe you're afraid to tell your friends about Jesus. Be brave like Esther.

Lord, make me brave to speak up when You call me to. Amen.

DAY 340

BEE-U-TI-FUL!

Your beauty should come from the inside. It should come from the heart. This is the kind that lasts. Your beauty should be a gentle and quiet spirit. In God's sight this is of great worth.
1 PETER 3:4

There are so many ways girls compare themselves to other girls. Truth is, if we look long enough, there will always be *that* girl. That girl whose hair is never messy, while ours is in a lop-sided ponytail. That girl who has a cute new T-shirt, while ours is a hand-me-down. That girl whose parents let her wear lip gloss, while ours don't. That girl who. . . You get the picture.

Ever wonder what God thinks about beauty? The most beautiful part of any girl isn't on the outside—her face, her hair, her clothes. Her real beauty is on the inside, in her heart. That's not how most people define beauty, and it might take some practice and some courage to change our own thoughts. But guess what? God can help us, and He is already making our hearts more beautiful every day.

God, help me see beauty like You do. Amen.

DAY 341

EVERY BIT

"Not one of the birds falls to the earth without your Father knowing it. God knows how many hairs you have on your head. So do not be afraid. You are more important than many small birds."
MATTHEW 10:29–31

A lot happens in a day. From the moment you roll out of bed in the morning until you jump back into bed at night, you do a lot, think a lot, see a lot, and feel a lot. Some things that happen are big, but most of our day is made up of small stuff. With so much going on, you may think, *NO WAY God keeps track of all this!*

The Bible tells us that nothing escapes God's eyes. A tiny bird isn't beyond His awareness or out of His control. And since He cares about you much, much more than birds, not even the tiniest detail of your life is unimportant to Him. With such a loving God who is taking care of absolutely every bit of you, what is there to fear?

Heavenly Father, You're looking after me, all of me. I won't be afraid! Amen.

DAY 342

LOVE ALWAYS

Love takes everything that comes without giving up. Love believes all things. Love hopes for all things. Love keeps on in all things. Love never comes to an end.
1 Corinthians 13:7–8

Love is a huge theme in the Bible. One of the most well-known verses, John 3:16, starts with "For God so loved the world. . ." *God loved us*—that's how God's grand plan to save sinners started. Love was at the beginning! And love is still first in our lives as Christians. Jesus tells us that the greatest commandment is to love God, and next to that is loving others (Matthew 22:37–40). Sounds simple enough, right? But love isn't so simple, is it? Especially loving people. When others are annoying or hurtful, you may want to run away from them instead! Biblical love, though, doesn't disappear. It keeps on. It never ends.

Need some help with love? (We all do!) First, remember God's love. Then face whatever comes with His love encouraging you.

**Lord God, Your love never quits.
Help my love to be like Yours. Amen.**

DAY 343

GOD-GIVEN

Moses said to the Lord, "Lord, I am not a man of words. I have never been. Even now since You spoke to Your servant, I still am not. For I am slow in talking and it is difficult for me to speak." Then the Lord said to him, "Who has made man's mouth? Who makes a man not able to speak or hear? Who makes one blind or able to see? Is it not I, the Lord? So go now. And I will be with your mouth. I will teach you what to say."

Exodus 4:10–12

God's plans for us don't always lead where it's comfy. God asked Moses to speak to Pharaoh, and that was waaaay outside Moses' comfort zone. Even though Moses answered with fear—"Me? Talk? But I'm not good at that, Lord!"—God told Moses that He, God Almighty, would give Moses the ability. So if God asks you to stretch and grow or serve Him in new ways, rely on Him. He is the one who gives you the ability—and the courage.

Lord, I'll trust in You wherever You lead. Amen.

DAY 344

STORMY WEATHER

God is our safe place and our strength. He is always our help when we are in trouble. So we will not be afraid, even if the earth is shaken and the mountains fall into the center of the sea, and even if its waters go wild with storm and the mountains shake with its action.

Psalm 46:1–3

Are you afraid of thunderstorms? It can be pretty scary when the sky gets dark and rumbles. Maybe tornadoes (or earthquakes or wildfires or hurricanes or floods) happen where you live, and just thinking about them makes you nervous.

Take another look at today's verses. The psalmist describes some frightening scenes. Can you imagine an earthquake so powerful that whole mountains fall into the ocean, or a storm so bad that wild waves cause mountains to visibly shake? Yet *even if* those things happened, there's no reason to fear! God is our safe place and help in every trouble, from thunderstorms to the worst natural disaster. He is our courage even then.

God, the scariest things aren't so scary— because You are with me! Amen.

DAY 345

FEAR GOD?

But the loving-kindness of the Lord is forever and forever on those who fear Him.
PSALM 103:17

You've read a lot about not being afraid. So what does the Bible mean when it tells us to fear God?

Fearing God isn't the same as being afraid of, say, a shark swimming straight toward you in the ocean. God loves and protects His kids. But as God's kids, fearing Him means that we never forget that He is God—He is awesome and powerful and holy, and therefore He is worthy of worship and respect. Fearing Him means being obedient to Him because He has the right to make the rules. Fearing God is good for us too! Proverbs 14:26–27 says, "There is strong trust in the fear of the Lord, and His children will have a safe place. The fear of the Lord is a well of life." This kind of fear doesn't make us cowering bundles crouching in a corner. No! It gives us courage as we live each day shielded by God's loving-kindness.

Lord God, show me how to fear You. Amen.

DAY 346

GOODBYE, WORRIES!

Give all your worries to Him because He cares for you.
1 Peter 5:7

Have you ever had a problem and you kept thinking about it and thinking about it? Or have you ever been nervous about something, and that one thought became stuck in your mind? Don't you wish you could just get rid of the worries? Well, that's exactly what God wants you to do! This verse tells us to give every worry to God. Other Bible translations say to "cast" our worries. There's no way we can carry them by ourselves, so we toss them to God. He's powerful enough to shoulder our troubles and support us too. Psalm 55:22 says, "Give all your cares to the Lord and He will give you strength. He will never let those who are right with Him be shaken." You can be fearless when you give your worries to God! Believe that He will take care of those worries, just as He's caring for you.

Lord, take these worries and fill me full of courage instead. Amen.

DAY 347

GPS

Your ears will hear a word behind you, saying, "This is the way, walk in it," whenever you turn to the right or to the left.
Isaiah 30:21

If you've ever ridden in a car with a navigation system or GPS, you can guess how easy it makes driving in an unfamiliar place. The driver doesn't have to worry about forgetting where to turn or not seeing a street sign. A voice tells her, "Turn right!" or "Turn left!" Wouldn't it be great if life had GPS? Whenever you had to make a choice, a voice would tell you, "Do this!"

As Christians, we do have guidance in our lives. God's Word guides us in how to live, and God Himself guides us each day. God is so awesome at guiding His kids that they don't even have to see where they're going to follow Him. He promises, "I will lead the blind. . .in paths they do not know" (Isaiah 42:16). So keep reading your Bible; keep listening for God's directions. When you stick close to Him, you can take each step bravely!

God, I'm never lost with You! Show me Your way. Amen.

DAY 348

THIS LITTLE LIGHT

"Men do not light a lamp and put it under a basket. They put it on a table so it gives light to all in the house. Let your light shine in front of men. Then they will see the good things you do and will honor your Father Who is in heaven."
MATTHEW 5:15–16

When you turn on a lamp, you wouldn't put it under something. That's pointless! You want the light to light up the room.

Believers have a purpose like that lamp. Jesus says to "let your light shine," but letting our light shine is never about us—it's about the one who gives the light. We can show bits of who God is to a world that doesn't know Him, just by living godly lives. We can bring light (things like truth and hope) to our homes and schools and neighborhoods, just by being like Jesus, who is the light of the world. Letting your light shine will take courage. You might be the only light. But even one little light can make a difference.

God, shine through me so people will see Your light. Amen.

DAY 349

FOR GOOD

"You planned to do a bad thing to me. But God planned it for good, to make it happen that many people should be kept alive, as they are today. So do not be afraid."
GENESIS 50:20–21

Joseph's brothers were shaking in their sandals! Years before, they threw Joseph into a pit and then sold him as a slave. Now they were standing in front of Joseph, and he wasn't their pesky little brother anymore—he was a very powerful man in Egypt. They were afraid that Joseph would want to punish them for what they had done. But Joseph said that God had taken the bad thing and made it good.

God still makes good come from bad. Romans 8:28 says, "We know that God makes all things work together for the good of those who love Him." So even if we're in the middle of rotten things, we can be courageous, because we *know* that God works *all things* for our good. God is that great!

God, bad things scare me, but I can be brave because You're planning something good. Amen.

DAY 350

OUR GOOD SHEPHERD

"My sheep hear My voice and I know them. They follow Me. I give them life that lasts forever. They will never be punished. No one is able to take them out of My hand."
John 10:27–28

Sheep aren't known as the bravest creatures. They're woolly, baaing bundles that run every which way when they're scared. Sometimes they might wander away from the rest of the sheep and get into trouble. Enter the shepherd. The shepherd's job is to look after his sheep.

In the Bible, Jesus is called the good shepherd. That's because He looks after Christians, His "sheep"—only He cares for us even better than a human shepherd. He knows each one of us individually and stays near us no matter what. Danger doesn't make Him run—in fact, Jesus conquered death so that we could live forever. Whenever you're feeling timid, think about Jesus. We are safe with our shepherd, and *nothing* can change that!

**Lord, thank You for shepherding me.
Thank You for giving me courage. Amen.**

DAY 351

NOT OUR WILL

He went on a little farther and got down with His face on the ground. He prayed, "My Father, if it can be done, take away what is before Me. Even so, not what I want but what You want." . . . He went away again the second time. He prayed, saying, "My Father, if this must happen to Me, may whatever You want be done."
MATTHEW 26:39, 42

Jesus is the ultimate example of courage. Before He died on the cross, He prayed to His Father multiple times. He wondered if there was another way to save sinners. Jesus was completely God, but He was completely human too, and He didn't want to go through the agony of paying for every single sin. *But* He chose to obey His Father anyway. He was courageous to say, "Your will be done."

How about you? When God's will means going through or doing things you'd like to skip, what will you say?

Heavenly Father, when Your will is hard, I want to do my own thing. Help me obey. Help me be courageous. May whatever You want be done. Amen.

DAY 352

A HELPING HAND

With Your help I can go against many soldiers.
With my God I can jump over a wall.
PSALM 18:29

What's the toughest thing you've ever had to do? King David, who wrote Psalm 18, had to do a ton of difficult things in his life. He had many enemies, and many times it probably seemed like those enemies would destroy him. So what did David do? He called out to God. That was the key to David's success and his courage: He knew he could only do the most difficult things *with God* helping him. "For Who is God, but the Lord?" David wrote. "It is God Who covers me with strength and makes my way perfect. He makes my feet like the feet of a deer. And He sets me on my high places. He teaches me how to fight, so that I can use a bow of brass. . . . Your right hand holds me up. And Your care has made me great" (Psalm 18:31–35).

God, I can do really hard things with Your help. I praise You! Amen.

DAY 353

A COURAGEOUS SPIRIT

For God did not give us a spirit of fear. He gave us a spirit of power and of love and of a good mind.
2 Timothy 1:7

When God makes us His kids, He implants "a spirit of power and of love and of a good mind." Sounds great! But what does it really mean? Take a look at two of those qualities—power and a good mind. Power in this verse means that we're able to deal with every hard thing and stay strong, because God provides everything we need to get through. A good mind means that we can think clearly about what's going on in our lives and stay calm, because we trust in God. Put simply, God didn't give us cowardly spirits—we're designed to be courageous! And these qualities of power and a good mind are already yours. It may not always *feel* like it, but inside you, your spirit is hardwired for courage.

God, I can be a courageous girl because You created me that way! You are an awesome God! Amen.

DAY 354

ALWAYS PRAY

Jesus told them a picture-story to show that men should always pray and not give up.
Luke 18:1

Jesus' story went like this: In a town there was a widow and a judge. The widow had a problem, so she kept asking the judge to do something about it. But the judge was a wicked man. He didn't care about God, and he didn't care about people, so he kept saying no. One day, though, the judge changed his mind. He was so tired of the widow bothering him that he decided to say yes and help her.

Jesus teaches us to pray and not give up because God is the opposite of that judge. If a wicked man did a good thing, how much more will God, who is totally fair and totally compassionate? He won't say, "Scram!" and He won't plug His ears, ever. It still takes guts to keep your head up and keep praying when things aren't going your way. But know that God is listening. And He will help.

**God, I'll never stop praying!
Thank You for hearing my prayers. Amen.**

DAY 355

UNCHANGING

Whatever is good and perfect comes to us from God. He is the One Who made all light. He does not change. No shadow is made by His turning.
James 1:17

Do you like changes? Some people love them—a change means something new! Other people want everything to stay the same. Like it or not, though, change happens. Just think—you start a different grade at school each year. Maybe your parents got divorced, or a younger sibling was born or an older one is about to go to college. You might move to a new city. You make new friends. And as you grow up, you do all kinds of new things. Those are only a few examples, but no matter how many things change in your life, and no matter whether the changes are exciting or scary, one thing stays the same: God. He is *immutable* (a big word that means God doesn't change). You can count on Him and find courage in Him always.

**God, You are so great and good—
and that will never change! Amen.**

DAY 356

TRUST HIM

Trust in the Lord with all your heart,
and do not trust in your own understanding.
PROVERBS 3:5

Has this ever happened to you? You're reading your Bible or listening to a sermon, and a verse pops out at you. You're excited about what it says. Then you close your Bible or walk out of church, and actually doing what the verse says isn't as easy as you think. Real-life stuff gets in the way. So you start to doubt. You try to figure it all out on your own. That's why today's verse is so important, even when it comes to courage. You have to trust God deep, deep down because sometimes your mind will tell you things like, *God says, "Don't be afraid," but going to the doctor's office is terrifying!* Or *God wants me to be bold about my faith, but what if the other kids think I'm weird?* In those situations—in *every* situation—trust God with your whole heart.

God, I can't always trust what goes on in my head, but I can trust You in my heart. Amen.

DAY 357

LOVE WITHOUT END

For I know that nothing can keep us from the love of God. Death cannot! Life cannot! Angels cannot! Leaders cannot! Any other power cannot! Hard things now or in the future cannot! The world above or the world below cannot! Any other living thing cannot keep us away from the love of God which is ours through Christ Jesus our Lord.

Romans 8:38–39

It's a classic plot in movies and books. Boy and girl meet. Boy and girl fall in love. Boy and girl live happily ever after. *Aahhh.* But in real life (sometimes even in movies and books), people "fall out of love." Something happens and the happy couple stop loving each other. The once-beautiful love story ends. *Ugh.*

But God's love is never-ending! Nothing—absolutely nothing—can take away His love. "Yeah," you might say, "but how about when I'm a crabby, sinful, unlovable mess?" Nothing—absolutely nothing—can stop His love for you. Let that love story encourage you today.

God, Your love is mine forever, and that makes me so happy. I love You too! Amen.

DAY 358

OUR DEFENSE

Shadrach, Meshach and Abed-nego answered and said to the king, "O Nebuchadnezzar, we do not need to give you an answer to this question. If we are thrown into the fire, our God Whom we serve is able to save us from it. And He will save us from your hand, O king. But even if He does not, we want you to know, O king, that we will not serve your gods or worship the object of gold that you have set up."

DANIEL 3:16–18

Shadrach, Meshach, and Abed-nego worshipped God, so they disobeyed King Nebuchadnezzar's command to bow down to his gold statue. The king gave them one last chance. He probably figured he had them beat, because what god could save them from his blazing-hot furnace? But the courageous trio didn't give in to the threats. They trusted God so fully with their lives that they didn't need any other defense but Him. God could save them if He chose. (He did save them!) They'd worship Him no matter what.

God, You are my defender. I can face anything that happens with courage. Amen.

DAY 359

GOOD PLANS

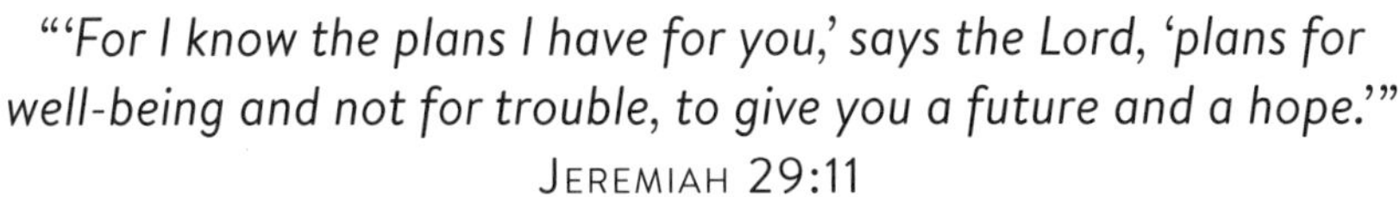

"'For I know the plans I have for you,' says the Lord, 'plans for well-being and not for trouble, to give you a future and a hope.'"
JEREMIAH 29:11

Today's verse is part of a letter that the prophet Jeremiah wrote. A group of God's people had been sent from Jerusalem to live in Babylon. They didn't want to be there. They'd much rather have returned home. But instead of sulking or becoming discouraged, they were supposed to carry on living their lives. God's instructions included building houses, planting gardens, and raising families. Most importantly, God wanted them to keep their minds on Him and His promises. Despite what anyone else might have said, He had good plans for them.

As Christians, we're here on earth temporarily, for a blink of the eye, until we live forever in heaven. Sometimes this life is hard. Sometimes we feel stuck where we don't want to be, like the Israelites. But God's advice is still the same: "Keep your mind on Me. My plans are good!"

God, when I'm losing my courage, I'll think about You and how You have good things planned. Amen.

DAY 360

TRACK RECORD

David said to Saul, "Let no man's heart become weak because of him. Your servant will go and fight with this Philistine."
1 SAMUEL 17:32

There he stood—Goliath. A mighty warrior, over nine feet tall, with brass armor and a huge spear. He was so terrifying that none of the men in Israel's army would fight him! On the outside, David was just a young shepherd. So when David said he would fight Goliath, Saul probably thought, *Yeah, right! Goliath will squish you like a bug!* Where did David get the courage to do such an incredible thing? While watching his sheep, David had seen how God helped him fight off wild animals. God would help him fight Goliath too. He told Saul, "The Lord Who saved me from the foot of the lion and from the foot of the bear, will save me from the hand of this Philistine" (1 Samuel 17:37). When *you* need courage, be like David and look at your life. How has God helped you before? He will help you again.

God, remind me of all the things You've done for me! Amen.

DAY 361

COURAGE FAIL

The Lord said, "Simon, Simon, listen! Satan has wanted to have you. . . . But I have prayed for you. I have prayed that your faith will be strong and that you will not give up."
LUKE 22:31–32

"Be courageous!" That's what God says, and we find a lot of examples in the Bible of courageous people. But sometimes we mess up because we act courage-less, not courageous. What then?

Peter (also called Simon in the Bible) messed up majorly. He once declared that he would never ever say he didn't know Jesus. Then Jesus was arrested. Peter was put on the spot. His courage failed. . .and he ended up saying three times that he didn't know Jesus. Peter was shocked and very upset by his actions, but Jesus knew all along what Peter would do. And you know what? Jesus loved him still. He had big plans for Peter's life, mistakes and all. He gave Peter—and He gives us—so much grace!

Lord, I'm not always so courageous, but You love me just the same. Help me be braver. Amen.

DAY 362

FORGET ME NOT

"Can a woman forget her nursing child? . . .
Even these may forget, but I will not forget you."
Isaiah 49:15

Does anyone like to be forgotten? Probably not! Being remembered makes us feel special. Being forgotten makes us feel tiny, unimportant. God's promise to His kids is that He will not forget us. And more than that, He knows us backward and forward—everything there is to know! Here's how the psalmist described God: "O Lord, You have looked through me and have known me. You know when I sit down and when I get up. . . . You look over my path. . . . You know all my ways very well" (Psalm 139:1–3).

Of the billions and billions of people in the world, God knows *you* just as completely. He is watching over *you* with just as much attention. So step into today with confidence and courage, girl! You are never forgotten!

God, sometimes I feel left out and forgotten by people, but I'm special to You! Thank You for caring about me so much. Amen.

DAY 363

GOD-DEPENDENT

"I have told you these things so you may have peace in Me. In the world you will have much trouble. But take hope! I have power over the world!"
John 16:33

As people grow up, they want to do more and more things on their own—to be independent. This desire for independence is good, but sometimes we can start to think that we are able or should be able to do everything by ourselves. Yet when it comes to spiritual things like courage, we just can't!

When Jesus warned the disciples that the world was full of trouble, He didn't tell them to buck up on their own. He said they could find peace *in Him*. They could take hope, or be courageous, because *He* has power. Courage (and every other part of being a Christian) isn't a do-it-yourself project. We need God to do it in us. So, as Hebrews 12:2 says, "Let us keep looking to Jesus. Our faith comes from Him and He is the One Who makes it perfect."

Lord, I need You every day.
Do amazing things in me, I pray! Amen.

DAY 364

HE'S GOT YOU COVERED

"Be sure you do not hate one of these little children. I tell you, they have angels who are always looking into the face of My Father in heaven."
MATTHEW 18:10

Maybe you've heard the term *guardian angel*. Some people believe that every Christian has one angel assigned to protect them. According to Jesus' words in today's verse, Christians have a whole team of angels! And those angels are always ready to come to our aid as soon as God commands.

Spend a few minutes thinking about these verses, and feel your courage grow:

- "Are not all the angels spirits who work for God? They are sent out to help those who are to be saved from the punishment of sin" (Hebrews 1:14).
- "He will tell His angels to care for you and keep you in all your ways. They will hold you up in their hands. So your foot will not hit against a stone" (Psalm 91:11–12).

Heavenly Father, You look out for me in amazing ways! Thank You! Amen.

DAY 365

"I'M WITH YOU!"

"I am with you always, even to the end of the world."
Matthew 28:20

Jesus met with His disciples in Galilee and gave them a job, what we now call the Great Commission: "Go and make followers of all the nations. Baptize them in the name of the Father and of the Son and of the Holy Spirit. Teach them to do all the things I have told you" (Matthew 28:19–20). Back when Jesus first called the twelve, He said He was sending them out "like sheep with wolves all around" (Matthew 10:16). Whoa! This task would be difficult too. So He ended His instructions with the encouraging words that He would be with them every step of the way.

The absolute best thing you can do with your life is use it to share God's good news. Tell others about Jesus. Live for God. And if the task ahead seems intimidating, remember the words of your helper and friend: "I am with you always, even to the end of the world."

Lord, may I be a courageous girl so everyone will know You! Amen.

CONTRIBUTORS

Jessie Fioritto (Days 1–61) is a work in progress for Jesus, homeschooling mom, and freelance editor and writer who does life alongside her husband and three spunky daughters.

Rae Simons (Days 62–122) is the pen name of a gifted, inspirational author from New York.

Janice Thompson (Days 123–183 and 245–305), a full-time author living in the Houston, Texas area, is the mother of four married daughters.

Hilary Bernstein (Days 184–244) is a Christ follower, wife, homeschooling mama, and writer who loves helping Christian women through her blog, hilarybernstein.com.

Linda Hang (Days 306–365) is a freelance editor who enjoys kayaking and discovering each day what God has planned for her—like writing books!

SCRIPTURE
INDEX

OLD TESTAMENT

Proverbs

NEW TESTAMENT

Matthew

Mark

Luke

John

1 John

Revelation

CHECK OUT THIS FUN FAITH MAP!

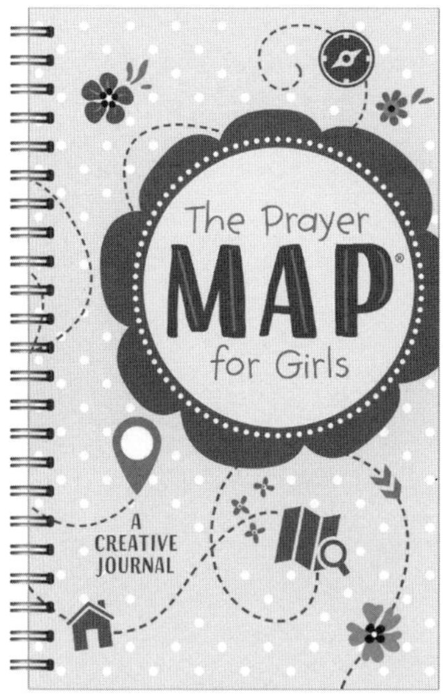

The Prayer Map for Girls

This prayer journal is a fun and creative way to fully experience the power of prayer. Each page guides you to write out thoughts, ideas, and lists. . .creating a specific "map" for you to follow as you talk to God. Each map includes a spot to record the date, so you can look back on your prayers and see how God has worked in your life.

Spiral Bound / 978-1-68322-559-1